SPEAKIN

TRAN

MW00916381

BY MARYSE CARDIN

ISBN-1974404382

Book cover by Avital David
Headshot photography by Cecile Gambin

Published by Dandelion Winds Press

For Robert and Eloise

I love you big time

and

For Hoben

For kindly teaching me again and again to just sit with
myself

What readers are saying about Speaking to Yourself with Love: Transform Your Self- Talk

I had the opportunity and honour to read a preview copy of Maryse Cardin's new book, *Speaking to Yourself with Love – Transform Your Self-Talk*.

This book is a road map to living your life with compassion, care and love – for yourself. There are a lot of us who have spent our lives helping and supporting others, and thinking about our own self-care may feel like a bit of an alien concept, but it is so important.

Many people have no idea about how much or how often they harm themselves with negative self-talk. For those who have lifted their heads – even a little – above the swamp of self-nastiness that we, as human beings, are so easily trapped in, this book is a lifesaver. If you take the guidance, advice and wisdom in this book to heart and you implement the tools that Maryse provides on every page, your life will change drastically for the better. –Ruth Atherley

Author Maryse Cardin's new book, "Speaking To Yourself With Love", creates for the reader an experience not unlike a one on one session with a supportive, loving coach. Love lives in her words. Each chapter begins with a stated intention, then teaches an aspect of self-love complete with colourful examples, many shared from the author's personal life experience with refreshing openness and honesty. Techniques and practices are then offered in clear and simple language, and we are encouraged to explore for ourselves how we can integrate them into our own lives. Self-talk is so powerful it can literally change your life for better or worse. Isn't it a blessing that, as Maryse writes, we get to choose what kind of self-talk we wish to create our lives with; and she makes it easy to learn how! – Kathleen Stuckert

In the book, Maryse beautifully weaves personal stories of her own experience with self-talk into practical step-by-step methods for acknowledging and changing your self-talk. Maryse's encouraging voice comes across to her readers like a warm hug - reassuring you that change is possible and that you can be kinder to yourself. I found the summary and questions at the end of each chapter helpful as they reinforced what you had just learned. Buy this book! Give yourself the powerful gift of speaking to yourself with love. – Amazon customer

Table of Contents

Introduction: Why I Wrote This Book

This old Japanese tale was told to me by my Zen Buddhist teacher, Hoben:

A man was walking down a country road in Japan. He saw in the distance his friend, Yusuke, riding a horse. As Yusuke got closer, it became evident that he was totally out of control. He wasn't holding the reins, his feet were not in the stirrups, and he swung wildly from side to side.

"Where are you going like that?" the man screamed out to his friend.

Yusuke replied, "I don't know. Ask the horse."

My self-talk once felt a lot like Yusuke's horse ride. It was out of my control. I was the recipient of whatever conversation my mind decided to have with me that day. It could be a wild, unpleasant, and sometimes downright cruel ride.

Like Yusuke, I did not know that all I needed to do was to grab on to the reins and put my feet in the stirrups to have a much more peaceful and controlled ride—whether the horse was wild or calm.

Speaking to Yourself with Love is a skill that you can learn. It is a choice you can make. You can choose to slow down in your life, and transform your self-talk.

Do you use words that put love in, that elevate you, or do you use words that put you down, that suck love right out of you like a leak in a tire?

Self-talk as a choice

Loving self-talk really is a practice. At the beginning, it feels unnatural because it is not the way many of us speak to ourselves. We have internalized voices since our childhood that may have been critical, bullying, unloving, harsh, pushy, or telling us that we are worthless unless we are perfect—like that's something humans can ever be. We have been told that we are bad, unlovable, stupid, or not good enough as we are. At the beginning, speaking to yourself with love can go against all that you have been hearing inside yourself for a long time. With practice, it gets easier, until finally it becomes your natural way of being.

My heartfelt intention with this book is for it to open up a door for you—or even a crack—into self-love as you choose to change the way you speak to yourself.

As we feel more love and compassion for ourselves, it radiates out to what we feel for others. The transformation begins with us, but it can extend to all the people in our lives, and then to all the people in the world.

How it started for me

Before, I didn't know that I got to choose how I spoke to myself. I didn't know that I got to decide how much compassion, kindness, understanding, and love could be in my life if I took hold of the power I have to give these things to myself. Just like I choose how I will speak to others, I get to decide how I will honour, love, and respect myself with my words.

I woke up one morning in my apartment and immediately let myself have it. I had been out the night before at a dinner party, had a few glasses of wine, and come home late. Nothing too extravagant, but still, my inner bully went berserk. "How could you? What is the matter with you? Look how tired you are. The whole day is shot. You can't do anything right. I can't trust you."

This was not an unusual voice to wake up to, but the difference that morning is that I suddenly heard what I was saying to myself. It appalled me. The voice was so dismissive, cruel, and critical. If anyone else had spoken to me that way as I first opened my eyes, I would have told them to shut up or leave.

For the first time, I decided to protect myself. I told myself to stop it, and that this voice had no right to speak to me this way. Amazingly, it stopped. It was my first realization of how mean I could be to myself, and that I had voices inside. More importantly, I realized that I could have some control over what they said.

Self-talk as a gateway to self-love

Learning self-talk skills was about learning to love myself. As we all have, I had heard much ado about self-love, but for me it remained abstract; I didn't really know what it truly meant or how to give it to myself. But communication, I understood. My career has always been about communication: studying it, practicing it, writing about it, researching it, and teaching it at universities. Self-talk became the gateway for me to self-love because I understand how powerful and transformative communication can be.

As I began to speak to myself with more kindness and compassion, and began listening to myself, I started feeling more love for myself. My relationship with myself began transforming. I started trusting myself more. I became less interested in pushing myself tirelessly to be perfect or to achieve, and more interested in standing by myself at all times. It worked exactly the same way as it does when I am building a friendship with someone: it is built on listening to the person, and treating them with kindness and compassion.

Each chapter explores a topic that leads you to speaking to yourself with love. Each is like a gateway to self-love. I invite you to slow down and spend time with the chapters that appeal to you. You can take your time and explore each chapter, or you can settle peacefully on just one or two. There, you can begin to look into your own heart and explore what it means to speak to yourself with love.

I have laid out the chapters to my own fancy, but by all means follow yours. Go ahead and skip from one chapter that calls your name to another. This is, after all, your own beautiful journey – and thank you for sharing it with me.

With loads of wishes for self-love and happiness,

Maryse

Chapter 1

There's Only Love, Only Love, Only, Only Love

Or Choose Words Of Love And Compassion

Our intention, together, in Chapter 1 is to choose words of love and compassion in our inner speech. By slowing down and spending time on this chapter, you are on the journey to Speaking to Yourself with Love.

To practice compassionate and loving self-talk is to give yourself the gift of words that show you care, and that are filled with mercy, empathy, and tenderness. It is your birthright to be spoken to with compassion and love—no matter who you are, what you have done, or what has happened to you. The more negative, cruel, and judgemental your regular self-talk is, the more you are in need of deep compassion and love. Wonderfully, you have the power to give this to yourself with your self-talk.

My story: Compassionate self-talk as a path I choose to take

There is a beautiful labyrinth in my city that I visit every chance I get. When I walk the labyrinth and follow its way, I am free to take time for myself, to meditate, to think, to pray.

As I walked it recently with my friend, I felt so grateful that a group of individuals created this space. It is quiet and peaceful, and feels like a safe haven in the city. I can always hear myself and connect with myself in the labyrinth, and find solace, gratitude, and sometimes serenity and joy. The critical voice lifts when I am there and I can hear a voice of compassion. I can experience a deep concern and sympathy for myself, my failings, my mistakes, my suffering, and my confusion.

There was a time when I could only experience this way of being when I was in the labyrinth or at some retreat centre; it is certainly easier to do so there. But in more recent years, since I have begun speaking to myself with more compassion, I can find a safe harbour within myself almost anywhere.

Even in the midst of life's storms, as the waves gather strength and I feel like I might be swept away, I can go to that safe harbour inside. I can connect with the part of myself that is calm, compassionate, accepting, loving, and forgiving. My self-talk helps me find this space, and so does my meditation practice. Before, I would grasp desperately for anything I thought would keep me afloat. Now, the safe harbour I go to is in my heart, in my soul, in the deepest part of me. My inner speech is about making myself feel safe, loved, accepted, and connected. I speak to myself with as much love and compassion as I can, and it is making a big difference in my life. I am calmer and more accepting of myself and others, and I have more joy.

I choose the path of speaking to myself with compassion, and I when I fall off of it or take a detour away from it, I am gentle with myself. I feel compassion for the woman who has again lost her way. Then I find my way back. I do so again and again. There is always a way back to the path and I can always start again by choosing words of love and compassion.

My self-talk
- I choose to speak to myself with love.
- I am safe here with myself.
- I love you. I love you. I love you.
- I am always here for you.
- You are important to me.

The exploration: Choose words of love

Write a love note to yourself. You can use short sentences or just words. Write about what you love about yourself. Write also about why you are proud of yourself. Tell yourself how deserving you are of love, and how you will give yourself as much love as possible. If you find it challenging, imagine what you would write to someone else whom you really love, then write those things to yourself. Start with "Dear" and end with "I love you." Sign your love note, and then read it to yourself. Here's mine, for inspiration:

Dear Maryse,

- *You are compassionate.*

- *I love you for being kind.*

- *I love you for caring for me.*

- *I love your sense of humour.*

- *I love you because you try to do what is right.*

- *I love that you see beauty in the people you love, and in the world.*

- *You are courageous and protect yourself and your family.*

I love you,

Maryse

Go ahead, give it a go! It may feel a little strange at first to write these words of love to yourself, but part of you will love hearing it.

Wise words

"To be beautiful means to be yourself. You don't need to be accepted by others. You need to accept yourself." –Thich Nhat Hanh

A story that inspires me

Maggie Howell – "It's okay to love myself and my life."

When Maggie Howell was a young girl, her mother said to her, "I am surprised you have any friends with the way you behave." That stuck and stayed with Maggie for years. For most of her adult life, her self-talk was negative and focused on controlling her actions so that others would like her. She never quite felt good enough. Then, one day in her early 30s, she realized that the way she spoke to herself was ridiculous.

She said to herself, "I am a nice person. What is the point in carrying on with that same self -talk?" Maggie explains, "That was a conscious decision I made on that day, and from that moment on I began to talk to myself in a different way. I have even get gotten to a point where, if I have done something well, I feel okay to say to myself, 'You are amazing.'"

She adds, "One of the self-talk practices that I use is to I remind myself that I have created this life. I have made this happen. My decisions have led me to this moment. This is my life. And what that does is make me realize that I am doing well, that I make good choices. That it is okay to love myself and my life. This works particularly well when I'm having a hard day or thinking that I'm not achieving or succeeding as much as I would like to."

When Maggie Howell was pregnant with her first baby (she now has five boys!), she brought her self-talk to the next level when she studied self-hypnotism for pain management and relaxation in preparation for child birth. She discovered how powerful her self-talk could be, and what she could accomplish by being focused on how she spoke to herself. Amazed by the results, she created her own hypnotherapy program. Now Maggie is a leading authority on positive self-talk and belief transformation for childbirth and fertility. She created Natal Hypnotherapy and has helped over 100,000 women through her classes, guided meditations, and videos. Her method is also widely utilized for general health and stress management.

Maggie is a great believer that we are not slaves to our self-talk. "Just because your self-talk has followed a certain pattern for many years, it does not mean it always has to be that way. Once you become aware of the potential power of how you speak to yourself and have the tools to change it, then everything in life becomes easier."

My story: The mothership, and embracing the good in the darkness

It is often the case that when I write about a subject, I get an invitation from life to explore it further and to heal what wants to be healed. One day I began writing on the subject of holding all of me—the parts I love, and the parts that I would rather be without. Later that day, I completely lost my temper with another mom in my daughter's kindergarten class after her son hit my daughter. I proceeded to spend the next few days ashamed that I hadn't been able to control myself. Ouch. Talk about an invitation to dive back into this subject.

Jung called the parts of ourselves that we would rather ignore and deny our "shadow self." They are the aspects that we keep hidden, deep down. The thing is, when they are held down, the resulting pressure can make them pop back up like a beach ball kept under water.

I am just starting to explore my shadow self. There are parts of me down there that I am inviting back up for air so that I can live in more harmony with them. In the darkness, I am finding some gems. As Marion Woodman wrote, good things can grow in the darkness, like roots, dreams, and babies.

As they say, "Own it." These are all parts of me: the grizzly Maryse with the explosive temper—she showed up in the kindergarten class. The anxious Maryse, who freaks out when she thinks she will be late. The Maryse who gets overwhelmed by being around too many people. The Maryse who is super bossy, and can bulldoze her way through life. The fun Maryse, who likes to drink wine and Greek dance in the town square on sunny days. The Maryse who gets hurt and disappointed and cuts people off. The Maryse who is disorganized and is so uninspired by housework.

I am trying to become more compassionate with all the Maryses. I sense that is where I will find more joy, healing, love, and freedom. I sense that as I love myself wholly, I will forgive myself more easily and forgive others, too. I am trying to become my own mothership —the base from which I live and hold all of me: the parts that I am proud of, and the parts that I am embarrassed by.

One woman realized, during one of my workshops, that she could not expect her husband to love all of her if she could not do that for herself. That is so very true for all of us.

As Dr Christiane Northrup wrote:

"No matter what you're feeling, the only way to get a difficult feeling to go away is simply to love yourself for it. If you think you're stupid, then love yourself for feeling that way. It's a paradox, but it works. To heal, you must be the first one to shine the light of compassion on any areas within you that you feel are unacceptable."

My self-talk

- It is okay to be who I am.

- I care for all of me and provide all of me with this strong, loving, and safe mothership.

- I can love all parts of me—the ones in the light and the ones in the darkness.

The exploration: Offer yourself words of compassion

Is there an area of your life, or a topic, in which you are particularly hard on yourself? Do you think your self-talk could use a little self-compassion, a hint of mercy, and a bit of tenderness? Self-compassion is to give yourself sympathy and tenderness for your hardships or failings—no matter what they are or who or what is causing them.

It is always really helpful to me when I'm able to get a sense of how I speak to myself. Once I know what I am saying to myself, I can choose to transform it.

Let me give you an example. I lost my temper with my daughter and felt such shame afterwards. My self-talk became very judgemental and cruel. Here are some of the words I said to myself:

- I am a bad mother.

- I can't control myself.

- I can't trust myself.

- I am a bad person.

When I stopped and realized what I was saying to myself, I extended a load of sympathy my own way— for being imperfect, for still learning how to speak to myself with love, and for how hard I judge myself. Here is what I chose to say to myself instead:

- I am sorry I spoke to you this way.

- I am doing my best.

- I am a good person.

- It's okay to make mistakes. I will be more patient next time.

- I am a good mother.

- You don't need to be perfect for me to love you. I love you as you are right now.

Now it is your turn. Pick a subject. For example, your health, your body, your relationship, your work, your friends. Write down some of the messages that you say to yourself in relation to the subject you choose.

Take some time to observe how you speak to yourself on this topic.

What would it be like if you decided to extend some compassion your way?

Now go ahead and cross out any messages that are hard, are unforgiving, don't support you, are cruel, or are just plain untrue. Cross them all out if necessary—you don't need them anymore.

Now, write yourself at least three messages that are filled with sympathy, compassion, understanding, and caring. Beautiful!

Wise words

"Use the word in the correct way. Use the word to share your love. Use white magic, beginning with yourself. Tell yourself how wonderful you are, how great you are. Tell yourself how much you love yourself." – Don Miguel Ruiz

In closing: A last exploration

I invite you here to take some time to write, doodle, or draw images of your impressions of this chapter. What inspires? What triggers you? What do you embrace? What are your intentions for your self-talk? Can you imagine speaking to yourself with more compassion, with more love?

Choose your next chapter in the journey

Bravo! You have begun choosing words of compassion and love in your inner speech. You can now choose to continue on the path that I've laid out and move on to Chapter 2. This next chapter is about speaking to yourself with kindness, like a very best friend would.

This is your journey. You can also choose to move on to a different chapter. Go where your inspiration takes you. Trust your inner voice. Where does it want to go?

Chapter 2

You've Got A Friend In Me

Or Choose Words Of Kindness

Our intention with Chapter 2 is to slow down, and choose words of kindness.

Just as it is in my power to decide to speak with kindness to my friends, I can choose to speak to myself that way, too. As Plato said, "Be kind, for everyone you meet is fighting a hard battle." That includes you, my sweet.

Think of how you feel elevated and connected when you see a friend you care about and they smile at you, ask you how you are, and really listen to the answer. Speaking with kindness to others brings them joy, comfort, calm, and acceptance. It makes them feel connected and less alone in this world. It gives them the strength to carry on. Our friends don't have to be perfect for us to speak to them that way. They can have problems and worries, they can make mistakes, and still we speak to them like a friend.

We want to speak to ourselves that way, like a real friend speaks to us. You have the power to comfort yourself, bring yourself joy, decrease your stress levels, and make yourself feel like you are not alone in the world—just by being kind and loving to yourself. As of now, meet your new best and dearest friend: you!

My story: Stand by me, what my cousin taught me about loving self-talk

Anyone who knows me well knows that I love my cousin Nathalie with all my heart. Her recent wedding was one of the most joyous days in my life. She is one of my best friends and I trust her fully. I also admire her.

That doesn't mean that I agree with all her decisions. Nonetheless, I have always stood by her no matter where a path took her in life, no matter what happened. I cannot fathom that I would ever turn my back on her or love her less.

It is very clear to me that I am there when she needs me. I also speak to her in such a way that it is clear to her that I love her. I speak to her with love even when I disagree with her. I speak to her with love even while being honest with her.

Lucky for me, she does the same for me. I know that when I finish telling her a story, no matter how embarrassing or in what a bad light it puts me, she will still be on my side. I remember sitting on a pier with her one day and telling her one such story. I was so filled with shame and disappointment that I could barely get the words out, but it was immediately clear to me that it changed nothing about how she felt about me.

My cousin is one of my most cherished friends also because of what she doesn't say to me. She doesn't bully me. She doesn't belittle me. She doesn't say hurtful things to me. She doesn't say or do these things because true friends don't act that way.

I have not always shown myself the kindness and love she shows me. I have turned my back on myself many times. I have made mistakes that I thought I could not self-forgive. I have left myself high and dry by refusing to be there for myself when I needed help or comfort. I have self-abandoned. I have ignored my needs to keep the peace.

Then I had a novel idea: What if I treated myself in the same way that Nathalie and I treat each other? What if I spoke to myself the way we speak to each other? My goal now is for my inner conversation to sound like my outer conversation with Nathalie.

To love is to accept yourself unconditionally, the way you are right now, right in the middle of what Jon Kabat-Zinn calls the "full catastrophe" that is our lives. With your self-talk, you can show yourself that you are not alone, that you are loved. When you build this relationship with yourself, when you show yourself that you can be trusted to have your own back or sit by your own sick bed, then you will never be alone again.

When times are hard or I have made a mistake, I will intentionally put my hand on my heart and speak to myself with love like my cousin does. I show myself with my words and my hand that I stand by me.

My self-talk

- I love you just as you are.

- You don't have to do anything for me to love you.

- I will stand by you through this.

- I am here.

- I believe in you.

The exploration: Becoming your new best friend

What do you say about spending a few moments exploring what it means to be a best friend? If you have a best friend, think of how you treat each other, what you say to each other, and how you feel when you are together. If you don't have a best friend right now, this is your opportunity to consider and imagine what qualities you would cherish in one.

How does your best friend talk to you? My best friend talks to me this way:

What is a message that your best friend has said to you that most made you feel joy? My best friend told me:

What is a message that your best friend has said to you when you needed comfort? My best friend told me:

What are things that your best friend would never say to you? My best friend would never say to me:

Now, spend a few moments thinking about what it would be like to choose to speak to yourself like a best friend.

Wise words

"I wouldn't trade it for anything. Never. No never. Your friendship is the best present ever." – Tigger

A story that inspires me

Sandra Bullock and self-kindness

A copy of People Magazine caught my eye at the dentist one day. There on the cover was Sandra Bullock, proclaimed as the most beautiful woman in the world. I was curious and pleased that the magazine picked a woman in her mid-forties. Finally, beauty is being celebrated at all the stages of life. I had to read the article.

In it, Sandra talked about how she wishes that her self-talk had been different when she was younger. She wishes that she had told herself not to worry so much and had spoken to herself with more kindness.

Here is a woman who seemingly has it all—beauty, fame, fortune, success, even an Academy Award for crying out loud— yet her concern is how she speaks to herself. She has learned that speaking to yourself with kindness is the most important thing you can do to be happy.

All those other things don't really matter if you don't speak to yourself with love and kindness. Self-talk truly is the great equalizer. There is nothing in your exterior life that will fill the void left inside if you self-criticize, put yourself down, and self-trash. There is nothing you can achieve that can heal the pain you put yourself through when you are unkind to yourself.

My story: Gently hold your own hand during hard stretches

As we all know, some weeks are more intense than others. Let me tell you about one of those. At one point in time, my daughter was sick with a respiratory ailment. I spent several sleepless nights holding her outside on the deck so the fresh air could reduce the swelling in her throat. Then I got sick too. By the end of the week I was barely keeping it together. The worry for my daughter, the lack of sleep and self-care… it all got to me. I found myself in the kitchen crying in the night, too tired and anxious to fall asleep. I couldn't think of anything else I could do to make things better.

And then it dawned on me, what I really needed. I needed someone to hold my hand. I needed to create a safe little harbour where I could begin to relax a little. I needed to show myself care and that I was not forgotten in all the events. I decided to do that for myself. I held my own hand with my self-talk.

I wrote myself a letter as I would to a friend going through a tough stretch. I told myself that I knew just how hard the week had been. That I was impressed with all that I had done and given that week. I wrote that I understood just how tired I was. I showed myself, with my words, that I got it. I gave myself a big dose of compassion and kindness. Then I gently encouraged myself. My daughter will soon heal, and I will soon sleep well again and feel better.

I also reminded myself of all the beauty and love that had happened that week: the lullabies I sang my daughter outside at night under the stars, the slow hours playing during the day, making art and planting flowers, the delicious Dahl a friend made me when she saw how tired I was, my husband going to work late so I could sleep a little in the morning. I felt grateful for all these showings of love, and took a few minutes to focus on them.

When I finished writing, I read the letter to myself. I breathed a huge sigh of relief at having been understood. It lightened my heart. I was then able to sleep after praying for healing for us both.

My self-talk

- I see how tired you are.

- I understand how difficult this is for you.

- Thank you for taking some time to connect with me.

- I really need some help. Thanks for giving it to me.

- I am here for you. I love you.

The exploration: Holding your own hand

Now it is your turn to hold your own hand. Is there an area of your life where you need to stand by yourself? Can you imagine what it would be like to hold your own hand? Make your intention to be there for yourself —to be present—with kindness and a big dose of love.

I want to stand by myself in this area:

I want to do this for myself:

I give myself permission to:

Wise words

"Be kind whenever possible. It is always possible." – Dalai Lama

In closing: A last exploration

I invite you here to take some time to write, doodle, or draw images of your impressions of this chapter. What inspires? What triggers you? What do you embrace? What are your intentions for your self-talk? Can you imagine speaking to yourself with more kindness? Can you think of yourself as your own best friend?

Choose your next chapter

In Chapter 2, you explored choosing words of kindness in your self-talk, being your own best friend, and holding your own hand. How beautiful! Well done!

You can now choose to continue on the path that I've laid out and move to Chapter 3. This next chapter is about the power our self-talk has in defining our own meaning. We get to choose—and to tell ourselves— what meaning every person and everything that happens has for us.

Again, this is your journey. If it better suits you, move on to a different chapter and pause there for a while. Go where inspiration takes you. Trust your inner voice. Where does it want to go?

Chapter 3:

It's My Life And I Get To Decide What It Means

Or Choose Words Of Meaning

Our intention with Chapter 3 is to choose words of meaning.

As the hero of your own story, you get to choose the meaning that each person, event, and outcome holds in your life. With your self-talk, you can help yourself understand what your life is about. It's all up to you, my sweet. For instance, you get to decide if the parting of ways with someone means failure, or a new beginning. You can choose what a hug means. You can decide if your life is about loving yourself and others as much as you can. It is your birthright to choose the meaning of your life—no matter what is happening.

Take a few moments to savour this poem, written by Wendell Berry, about a person whose life's meaning is to bring healing to our world by planting clover—a plant that restores health to depleted soil.

> In the darkness of the moon, in flying snow,
> in the dead of winter, war spreading, families

dying, the world in danger,
I walk the rocky hillside, sowing clover.

My story: A Hawaiian god and what my life means to me

I was at the hospital visiting my father, who was very ill, when I was given a symbol of joy and love. After a long, scary night keeping vigil by my father's bed, an orderly came into the room to get another patient. This attendant was wearing a tight t-shirt and pants, fashionable red glasses, a spiky haircut, and a huge smile on his face. He exuded joy and acted like it was the best thing to be there in the hospital, to be of assistance. Seeing him, the other patient began to smile. I began to smile. I was buoyed just by spending a few minutes across the room from this man. The meaning that I attributed to the orderly's visit was that there is joy and love in the hospital. He brought it to my awareness. Joy and love can exist hand-in-hand with terrible sadness.

This is a big freedom that I have: to be able to give meaning to all that I encounter in my life. I get to decide what people and events mean to me. When relationships end, I can decide what the person means to me, even if we don't speak again. My former business partner and friend, Frances, and I haven't spoken in years. We drifted apart after spending many years intensively in each other's company. When I think of her now, the meaning she has for me is friendship, love, adventure, trust, compatibility, growing up together, entrepreneurship, and fun—oh, did we have fun together. Whether we ever speak again changes nothing to what she means to me.

My friend Heidi is a talented artist, and a great believer in infusing meaning and symbolism into your life. She recognizes the signs that life gives us and shows great wisdom in deciphering them. I visited her in Hawaii after a hard breakup. I was tired of picking partners who did not hold their own. I was discouraged. Heidi gave me the wonderful gift of two statues she had sculpted. One was of the Hawaiian god Kū, whose name means "to stand," and the other his partner Hina. She told me that my next partner would be solid and strong like this god. I put it on my armoire and looked at it frequently. It guided me in choosing differently in my next relationship. When my future husband asked me out, I knew he embodied some of Kū's qualities.

These sculptures also represented love and support, as they were given to me by my dear friend. I will always be grateful to Heidi for showing me a way to find love. After my visit with her, I was no longer someone who failed at love. I was someone who hadn't yet gotten together with her mate. I was still on the journey towards love.

My self-talk

- I get to decide what this means to me.
- It is not what happens to me, it is what I decide to believe of it.
- This sculpture means love to me.
- This is meaningful to me.
- My life is filled with meaning. I am guided.

Your turn to explore: Animal symbols

Lately, I have been exploring the idea of animal symbols as a way to help me give meaning to how I am, who I am, and what qualities I want to strengthen in myself. These animals have come to me in meditation and by my observing them in nature. Sometimes, an animal calls my attention.

One evening, when I was taking a walk and feeling overwhelmed by life, I stopped for a moment and held my head in my hands. When I looked up again, there was a huge barred owl a few feet away, looking straight at me. He looked vigilant and yet so at ease in the growing darkness. I thought: This owl goes venturing out in the darkness unafraid. He sees things that others can't.

For some time after that, I saw owls everywhere: on book covers, in songs, on t-shirts. They kept coming up again and again. It reminded me to be more at ease in life and to stop being afraid of what I might find in the darkness.

Another animal guide that I have is the hummingbird. This funny little bird reminds me to lighten up. If I am feeling particularly sorry for myself, or dramatic, chances are that I will see a hummingbird that day. I say to myself, "Lighten up, my sweet girl. It's going to be okay."

I am also guided by the monkey. Monkeys don't give a rat's ass what others think of them; they are irreverent. They do their own thing. I want to be more like that. I say to myself, "I am like the monkey. I am myself. It is none of my business what others think of me."

Now it is your turn to find meaning in our animal friends. Use your imagination. Have fun!

Is there an animal that inspires you, or that you are curious about? What qualities does this animal have? How can these qualities help guide you? What can you say to yourself about how you are like this animal?

If you are inspired, draw your animal symbol(s). Be as creative as you would like.

Wise words

"When I am running on the seawall, I speak to myself the way Mohammed Ali spoke to himself. I imagine that he is the one speaking to me, encouraging me, telling me that I can run faster and harder. I am him when I run." – First Nations Elder Latash

A story that Inspires me

Cecile Gambin – "I tried to find meaning in it by learning and becoming a stronger athlete."

Very few careers are as black and white about winning and losing as professional sports. Athletes are trained to beat others and their own personal bests. When you win, you fly high, but when you lose, it can be crushing. Many athletes are well trained in utilizing self-talk to motivate themselves to train, and in visualizing winning competitions and games. On top of that, they also use positive self-talk when they lose, to find meaning in their defeat.

Cecile Gambin is now a photographer, teacher, mother of two active boys, and an off-road rider, but previously, she was a highly competitive and successful mountain biker specializing in downhill races. She was top of her field, medaling in Canada Cup events several times and competing internationally.

The pressure was on. Her sponsors expected her to win or place well, and to generate positive publicity for them. She also had the strain of the other up-and-coming athletes vying for her position. Self-talk helped her become a better athlete by learning from both her wins and her losses.

"Whether I won or not, I always looked at what I could do better—whether it was better preparation, more mental focus, or more fitness, etc. There was always room to learn, and to grow, and I would try and figure that out. I was disappointed when I lost—actually, it sucked. But I tried to find meaning in it by learning and becoming a stronger athlete. My losses played a role in my success. If I didn't win and I gave it my best shot, then I was okay with that. I can only do my best. I can't control what will happen after that."

She also used her self-talk skills to build her self-esteem, telling herself that she had what it took to be a racer.

"I probably put the biggest pressure on myself wondering if I was good enough to be on the team. I felt I had to prove myself—not just to others, but to myself. I told myself that if they hired me on the team, it was because they believed in me, and all I had to do was to believe in myself. That took some inner work because it is easier said than done. Self-doubt is a killer."

In everyday life, Cecile uses the self-talk skills that she acquired as an athlete, especially when there is some pressure and she needs to focus and do her best. She will tell herself, "Come on Gambin... you can do it!"

"I relate back to prior experiences and tell myself if I did it once, I can do it again. If it is a new experience, I still draw on past experiences to help calm myself," she adds.

Wise words

"What matters, therefore, is not the meaning of life in general but rather the specific meaning of a person's life at a given moment." – Viktor E. Frankl

My story: Make the story your own

When I was small, my father told me many stories about my grandfather, and how hard he worked. He was pulled out of school at eight years old to work with his stepfather. As a teenager, he shovelled coal into the furnace of a ship. Throughout the Great Depression, he was the only relative with a job, with two jobs, with three jobs. Whatever it took, whatever was needed, he did it. He kept the whole extended family afloat.

The job that I remember most was the one he took as a truck driver. You see, when my grand-father applied for the job, he didn't have a license and didn't know how to drive, but he was gutsy and determined. He taught himself how to do it. When he later left the job, his boss said he was sorry to see him go; he had been his best driver. My grandfather didn't know how to shift gears, so he drove the truck in first gear everywhere, very slowly, and very carefully. Turns out, he was the only driver in the company never to have an accident.

I told this story as a teenager to my friend Natsuko. She loved it, and still talks about it 30 years later. Many times, when she hit a wall in life and didn't know if she could succeed at something, she thought of my grandfather. She made the story her own. The story has meaning for her. "If he can do it, I can do it," she tells herself. Natsuko has a remarkable will. She is strong and courageous, but even she sometimes needs some encouraging self-talk. That is what my grandfather's story does for her. She relates to the story and the characteristics that my grand-father demonstrated: determination, hard work, courage.

My grandfather didn't just inspire Natsuko; he inspired me and helped me define myself. His story has meaning for me, too. After my father told me the story about my grandfather, he told me I was just like him— that I am courageous and don't give up easily. That is a part of my self-talk that I inherited, and that works for me. No matter what you tell me the odds are of doing something, I think I can do it. "It is possible," I tell myself! "Why not me?! I'll figure it out somehow!"

My self-talk

- I can choose to be a certain way and strengthen a quality in me.

- I get to make this story my own.

- I can do it.

- I can figure it out.

- Why not me?!

The exploration: A coat of arms to symbolise you

A coat of arms is a shield with symbols and figures on it which represent a person, family, group, or organization. I invite you to make one as a visual self-representation. Images and symbols help us to communicate with ourselves. With this coat of arms, you tell yourself about an important part of who you really are. You get to decide what is meaningful and important to you. You can also include qualities that you share with a person you admire.

My own coat of arms includes a pen for writing, waves for the healing effect that water has on me, a hummingbird as a symbol of light and play, a lion for courage, and a mother with her arms around her child, for the importance that motherhood—to my inner child as well as to my daughter—plays in my life.

Would you like to create your own coat of arms?

Choose at least four symbols that represent you: your beliefs, your loves, your strengths, your passions, your dreams, and your successes. You can draw your symbols (possibly even inside the traditional lozenge shape of a coat of arms), or write about them.

In closing: A last exploration

I invite you here to take some time to write, doodle, or draw images of your impressions of this chapter. What inspires? What triggers you? What do you embrace? What are your intentions for your self-talk? Can you imagine speaking to yourself in a way that helps you define what your life means?

Choose your next chapter

You have just spent important time pondering the meaning that you give your life with your self-talk. You have chosen words of meaning.

You can now choose to continue on the path that I've laid out and move to Chapter 4. This next chapter is about speaking to yourself in a way that demonstrates that you are more important than your problems. Our intention is to choose words that give us a sense of our own value and how cherished we really are.

This is your journey. You can choose to move on to a different chapter and pause there for a while. Go where inspiration takes you. Trust your inner voice. Where does it want to go?

Chapter 4:

I Am More Important Than My Problems

Or Choose Words Of Self-Worth

Our intention with Chapter 4 is to choose words of self-worth.

It's a big life, and sometimes you encounter big problems, or certainly a series of small ones to be overcome. It is easy to get lost in them—to forget that you have a whole inner world separate from what you are facing on the outside.

With your self-talk, you can keep yourself front and center and create that sense of separation between you and events. You can remind yourself of just how precious you are. You can communicate with that part of you that remains untouched. And you can remind yourself that this too shall pass.

My story: I am more important than my problems

When I had my PR agency, some days were very demanding with clients and journalists, employees and deadlines. At times, I would become completely enmeshed in the problems that arose there. If I made even one mistake in a day of 25 successes, if any of my clients were dissatisfied, or if a story generated negative media coverage, I would blame myself. It didn't matter whether the events were in or out of my control. It didn't matter whether what was asked of me was unreasonable. I criticized myself hard if I wasn't able to fix everything I encountered or keep everyone happy. I didn't have any separation from my work problems.

In the middle of one such stressful period, I read the line, "You are more important than your problems."

My goodness, what if that is possible? I know I am reading or hearing something that is true for me when my heart jumps up and down like an excited child. Yes! Yes! Yes! That is true!

This was the first time I recognized that I was separate from what I was experiencing on the outside. I was more important than the work challenges, relationship problems, tribulations, and little hiccups that happened in my life. "Yes! Yes! Yes! That is true," said my heart.

I remember one evening, swimming length after length in an outdoor swimming pool by the ocean, repeating that line to myself: I am more important than my problems. I am more important than my problems. I came out of that swim feeling calm, and that indeed part of me was untouched by what happened around me.

After that, I repeated the sentence to myself every time life became nerve-wracking. It was the beginning of a new way of looking at life and of talking to myself.

When I feel overwhelmed by life's challenges, when I have problems that worry me, I will remind myself that I am a separate being from the situation that I experience. There is a part of me that is always good and always pure, no matter what the situation. I want to make sure that I continue speaking to myself with love —because I am more important than my problems.

My self-talk

- I am more important than my problems.

- This too will pass.

- You made a mistake and I love you still.

- I will focus on myself and what is in my control.

- It is okay. I am okay.

Wise words

"Whatever is happening, whatever is changing, whatever is going or not going according to my plans—I release my hold on all of it. I leave behind who I think I am, who I want to be, what I want the world to be. I come home to the great peace of the present moment." – Elizabeth Lesser

The exploration: Lighten the load

Let's lighten the load caused by carrying our daily problems and challenges.

Let's begin with our intention: To tell ourselves how important we are at all times, no matter what is happening.

Put your hand on your heart and say three times: "I am more important than my problems."

A story that inspires me

Aviva Riley – "I told myself that I could prevail even under difficult circumstances."

My friend Aviva Riley once received a professional legal scholarship to attend a prestigious conference in New

Orleans. As the scholarship recipient, she was expected to attend a special reception as a guest of honour. It was a big deal. The problem was, though, she was feeling ill that day.

She sat in her hotel room, defeated, telling herself that she just could not get it together to attend. Then her toiletry bag caught her eye. On it was a cowgirl drawing her gun, and it read: "I am hit but I can make it." It had been a gift from a friend. (Full disclosure: me!)

"That message galvanized me," says Aviva. "I kept repeating it to myself. I told myself that I could prevail even under difficult circumstances." She got dressed and successfully attended the conference, fulfilling her obligations and making good professional contacts in the process, and, most importantly, being proud of how she helped herself rise to the occasion with her self-talk.

Wise words

"No problem can be solved from the same level of consciousness that created it. You must learn to see the world anew." – Albert Einstein

My story: Be on your own side, too, and show yourself kindness and compassion

A student came to see me during university office hours one day. She wanted to discuss the fact that her mother had been ill for years. This student, so young, was her mom's main caretaker, and they were presently going through a difficult spell. She wanted me to know that she would most likely be missing classes and deadlines. I was touched by her story, as I always am when I realize just how much responsibility some of my students shoulder.

As she continued to tell me her story, she began to cry. She put herself down, saying she just wasn't managing to do anything well. She was a perfectionist, she went on to explain. That word always raises a red flag with me. I take it to mean, "Nothing is ever good enough. I am not good enough."

Finally, I said, "It sounds like you have a lot of stress, and a lot of responsibility right now. How about being on your side? How about providing some kindness and compassion for that person taking care of her mother and going to school full time? Don't you think she needs love and kindness too?"

My student sat there looking at me for a long time. I could see that she had never thought of it that way.

Then she quietly said, "Yes, she does need love and kindness too."

I know how hard it is to remember to extend kindness and compassion to ourselves. We need some every day —and tons more when we are going through a hard stretch. Self-compassion and self-kindness are two of my practices, like yoga or meditation. I just keep trying to do it, even if I don't always see any progress.

A yoga teacher once told me not to worry if I fall over while trying to stand on one leg. "Just think of it as putting more balance inside yourself by doing the pose, instead of saying you don't have balance." In the same way, I just keep putting love in by practicing self-compassion and self-kindness.

My self-talk

- You are a good, kind person.

- You are doing your best in difficult circumstances.

- I am proud of you.

- I see how hard this is for you.

- I love you just the way you are.

The exploration: The Golden Message

This week, I had a big AHA moment, as Oprah likes to say. I realized that I sometimes tell myself that I am a bad person. The negative self-talk is there under the radar, almost like reading between the lines. It can happen when I don't get along with someone, or when I fail, or when I feel anxious. The bigger the problem I am facing, the more likely I am to say it to myself, especially if I can't seem to resolve it. It's a default setting within me.

Therefore, for me, the most kind, loving thing I can say to myself is: "You are a good person. I love you."

This is what I call the "Golden Message"—the one that I most need to hear, most long to hear from a loved one. It is a message of kindness I can say to myself.

What about you? Is there a Golden Message for you? What do you most long to hear? What will bring you relief? What will bring you joy? Go ahead and write your Golden Message.

Now put your hand on your own heart for a fuller connection with yourself, and say this Golden Message three times, or more if you are inspired.

In closing: A last exploration

I invite you here to take some time to write, doodle, or draw images of your impressions of this chapter. What inspires? What triggers you? What do you embrace? What are your intentions for your self-talk? Can you imagine reminding yourself that you are more important than your problems in your self-talk?

Choose your next chapter

In Chapter 4, we remembered that we are more important than our problems, and that we have the ability to connect with a place inside ourselves that is separate from it all, through our self-talk.

You can now choose to continue on the path that I've laid out and move to Chapter 5. This next chapter is about telling yourself the truth and accepting what it is. It is about the beauty in living with more harmony with what is.

This is your journey. You can choose to move on to a different chapter and pause there for a while. Go where inspiration takes you. Trust your inner voice. Where does it want to go?

Chapter 5

Tell Yourself The Truth Even When You Don't Want It To Be True

Or Choose Words Of Truth And Acceptance

Our intention with Chapter 5 is to choose words of truth and acceptance.

To be connected inside yourself with your own truth is an empowering way to be. To come clean with yourself, to tell yourself who you really are, what you really want, how you really want to live. Part of you sighs with relief when it is told the truth. With your self-talk, you can learn to stand with your head high in your own truth—no matter what it is.

Truth can also mean accepting "what is"—the reality of the moment. Accepting what is doesn't mean that you like it. It means that you don't fight against it or pretend that it isn't happening. It is about finding a way to live more peacefully with circumstances. It is that fine balance between being happy with what you have and still wanting to manifest your heart's desire.

My story: Accepting the truth even when you don't want it to be true

When my daughter was 18 months old, we went on a family holiday. Mid-way through the flight, she vomited, so I cleaned her and changed her clothes. No worries.

Then the vomiting really began.

It was like a scene out of a horror movie. She was so young and distraught that she hurled herself everywhere. By the time it was finished, we were both covered with vomit from head to toe, as were our seats and the airplane all around us. We sat there stunned. People around us gagged. I didn't have any more clean clothes for either of us.

Every part of my body and mind rejected this situation. Nooooo. I did not want to be on this airplane with my daughter having fallen sick. I did not want to be stinking and wet, still hours away from our destination. I felt tense and upset. Then I decided that, since I had no choice, I was going to accept my circumstances, even if I didn't like them at all.

"This is really disgusting and upsetting," I said to myself. "It is okay. You can handle this. For now, this is what is going on." Immediately, my shoulders relaxed and dropped two inches. I had accepted reality and the truth of my situation.

Letting the truth be the truth, even when I don't want it to be true, has been a long and steep learning curve for me.

I was standing in line for breakfast at a retreat centre some years ago, when I started talking to the woman behind me. We spoke about the importance of speaking your truth. It was so hard for me back then to stand in my truth and to fully be myself, and I told her so.

She responded with words that I still think about now: "When you speak your truth, your allies can recognize you and come forward." That woman was Gail Larsen, a coach, author, and founder of a great program called Transformational Speaking. I took a workshop with her sometime later to share in more of her wisdom, but those first words spoken to me in the lineup were the ones that stuck.

I have found that what Gail told me about truth is, well, true. It applies to what I say to others as well as to what I say to myself. When my self-talk is honest, whether it is listening to what my deepest truth is inside or admitting a truth that I have long been denying, something shifts. Part of me steps forward with relief, acknowledgement, excitement, or joy. I rally around myself, coming forward like an ally.

The truth is the truth, even if it isn't sensible, socially acceptable, popular, consistent with prior behaviour, or tidy. My truth is my truth, even when someone else dislikes it.

Most importantly, I have to hold sacred what I say to myself. I have to respect it and honour it. I must accept what I have said as true, even when I don't want it to be true.

And the airplane story? It had a happy ending. Fellow passengers came forward to literally lend us the clothing off their backs, to offer us medicine, napkins, and words of comfort and encouragement. We got off that flight looking like a ragtag bunch, but with much gratitude in our hearts for the sunshine and tropical breeze that greeted us at our destination.

My self-talk

- It is my birthright to have my own truth.

- I want to know what is true to me.

- I accept that this is my truth, even if I don't like it.

The exploration: What are some of your truths?

Being a safe harbour for yourself means becoming a place where you can be safe to tell the truth, where you will accept the truth for what it is with compassion. Your truth may be that you have outgrown some things or people in your life. You may want to make a different decision, or change your mind. You are allowed to tell yourself that it is okay to change and grow. The truth is like your roots, like your foundation: it may be underground, deep inside you.

These are some of the truths that I have admitted to myself in the past. Some were easy to tell myself, others hard. They come from the deepest part of me.

- "This person no longer loves me. I don't feel good around him anymore."

- "I don't want to be here."

- "I am not very good at this."

- "This friendship is finished."

- "I want to change."

- "I want to do something else with my work."

- "I need more time for myself."

In this exercise, I'd like you to look deep inside at some of the truths that you carry. What would you like yourself to know? What wants to come up to the light? This is about being truthful, not necessarily about taking any action about it. The truth is our foundation.

Wise words

"The thing you fear most has no power. Your fear of it is what has the power. Facing the truth really will set you free." – Oprah

A story that inspires me

Jacky Yenga – "Whenever I have the courage to look inside, I always know what feels right and what doesn't. If not, how can I make my life better?"

Jacky Yenga is a speaker, teacher, and performer. In her events and teachings, she helps people find their truths so that they have more connection to themselves and to others. Her events, like her African Healing Nights, are filled with delicious food, dancing, music, and laughter. You leave her events feeling joyous and uplifted, and knowing that you matter and you belong. Born in Cameroon and raised in France, she aims to bring African wisdom to the West.

Living truthfully is one of Jacky's core values. "I am upfront. I like for people to tell me the truth. I like to know where I stand. It's the same with my relationship with myself. I go as deep into the truth as I am aware of it. I aim to uncover what is hidden deep within myself and bring it to the surface. It is my responsibility to follow the truth. Whenever I have the courage to look inside, I always know what feels right and what doesn't. If not, how can I make my life better?"

Jacky connects into the truth of who she is through many practices, like meditation and prayer, but her main modality is African dance.

Says Jacky, "There is a lot of truth in dancing because you show up as you are. The more I practice dance, the more I find out about myself. It is like peeling an onion. I connect deeper and deeper into myself. I allow the dance to guide me. It can be uncomfortable, but the truth won't hurt me. The truth doesn't require you to like it, it just is. When I have ignored my truth, I have lived to regret it."

For Jacky, tapping into your truth is like exercising a muscle. It gets stronger with practice. "You work at it, and then you just know when it feels right, when you have hit the truth. It is not an intellectual pursuit, but rather a process of moving into alignment with your soul and body, where you have greater access to the truth of who you are at any given moment, as well as the truth of the universe. Because the body doesn't lie, and the soul doesn't lie. When you learn to listen and pay attention, you are literally having a conversation with your body and your soul. That's why dancing is so important to me. And when you develop a healthy relationship with your body and soul, you can be guided through life with greater wisdom. At least, this is what I believe and strive for, and this is what I love to teach," she adds.

My story: As good as it gets for now

There was a mom at my daughter's preschool who was a hospital physician working 12-hour shifts. She had three kids, one of whom was a baby. She also owned a horse, of all things, that she rode several times a week and cared for.

I have to admit that I was a little envious of her. Not of her life, but of her energy levels. I used to live like her, but I've never been built for it, and it was to the detriment of my health and well-being. The truth is that I need a lot more self-care and rest than the average person.

A few years ago, many of my big life dreams all came true at the same time: I had a child after years of wishing for one, I had a strong, loving marriage after a long stretch of failed relationships, I got the job I coveted at a nearby university, and I signed my first contract with a publisher and was writing my first book.

These were all good things, but I was stretched thin. I was busy beyond anything I had ever considered busy. I moved faster than ever just get it all done. I was constantly exhausted and wasn't sleeping very much. Around that time, a journalist friend asked me if I was enjoying writing the book and taking my time to craft just the perfect sentence. That made me laugh so hard, as I barely had time to whip out the sentences.

Overwhelmed by all these marvellous opportunities, I cut out what I thought was the least important: my self-care. I threw all that I had learned about the importance of caring for myself out the window, and of course, one morning my body said "no more." It literally shut down the operation. I was developing serious adrenal issues.

Anyone who has had adrenal problems knows that it feels like the batteries are taken right out of you, like the life force is drained. It worried me enough to make serious changes in my life. Step by step, I have been building my health back. I have been listening to my body and spirit and giving them what they need for well-being.

The truth is, there are still many things that I can't do. I just don't have the resources or stamina for them. I don't want this to be true, but I have come to accept it. (Well, most of the time anyway…)

A sage therapist once described to me a situation in which a mother-in law was visiting her son and daughter-in-law overseas. Within a few days, a quarrel had erupted and the mother-in-law refused to come out of her bedroom for the duration of the trip. "That is really sad," I said. "Not at all," he replied. "Under the circumstances, and knowing those people, that may have been the best-case scenario."

The best-case scenario is sometimes so far from our ideal, from how we want things to be, that we don't accept that it is okay. We are so attached to an idea or an expectation that we fail to see that things are as good as they can be right now. I try to remember this when something doesn't work, or I don't get along with someone, or I stand there finding nothing to say. When I am teaching and my students are distracted, no matter what I try. When I call someone by the wrong name. When water leaks through the ceiling in the living room. When the house is a mess again. When I forget to do something.

So many days fall short of my ideal. I can just do the best with this day and let go of my expectations.

Knowing me and knowing the circumstances, it's possible that they weren't realistic anyway.

There can be beauty in what is. If I take the time to look for it, I often find it. The truth is also that it has been really liberating to slow down, and to give myself permission to do less.

My self-talk

- It's okay to take my time.

- Pause now. I need some rest.

- I would like to say yes, but I need to say no. I just don't have the resources to do this right now.

- Maybe this is as good as it gets for now.

- You are doing your best. Just keep it up.

The exploration: As good as it gets for now

Can you think of a situation in your life where you are having trouble accepting the truth of it? Is there anything that you have been struggling with for a long time and that doesn't seem to change?

Imagine telling yourself that it is okay—no matter what is happening. That you know you are doing your very best, and that is all that you can do. Give yourself permission to be who you are and to feel what you do.

In this exercise, you are invited to write a message that reflects the beauty in what is.

In closing: A last exploration

I invite you here to take some time to write, doodle, or draw images of your impressions of this chapter. What inspires? What triggers you? What do you embrace? What are your intentions for your self-talk? Can you imagine speaking the truth to yourself? Can you imagine accepting what is?

Choose your next chapter

In Chapter 5, you looked at telling yourself the truth and accepting it. There can be beauty in what is.

You can now choose to continue on the path that I've laid out and move to Chapter 6. This next chapter is about choosing words of courage.

This is your journey. You can choose to move on to a different chapter and pause there for a while. Go where inspiration takes you. Trust your inner voice. Where does it want to go?

Chapter 6:

Saddle Up, Even If You Are Scared

Or Choose Words Of Courage

Our intention with this sixth chapter is to choose words of courage.

It's amazing what can happen when you are reminded to have courage. I was outside the hospital feeling scared to walk in to visit my father who was very ill. A friend supported me by simply saying, "Be courageous." It injected a big dose of courage into me. I wasn't told that there was nothing to fear; I was advised that courage would help me handle it. I felt more calm, more accepting of circumstances, more capable of facing them. I stood taller and walked into the hospital. I would be courageous in facing this time in my life and living through it with as much love and grace as I could muster.

To have courage doesn't mean there is an absence of fear, it means that we don't let fear stop us from doing what we know is right or what we are called to do. I have heard so many of my heroes say that they are scared; they just follow their calling anyway.

My story: Be courageous and take your boat out for a sail

One summer, I climbed a path of uneven stones up to a hilltop that has been a site of spiritual devotion for thousands of years. A church has stood there since the year 800, and before that pagans trekked up to worship the moon. There is a beautiful energy there, and the view of the Mediterranean Sea is stunning.

The church is called Notre-Dame du Bon Port, and it is devoted to the protection of the local fishermen. It is filled with marine regalia and objects, like wooden sailboats and paintings of ships at sea. The walls are covered with plaques, some giving thanks to the deities for bringing the sailors safely back to port during storms, and others in remembrance of the unlucky ones who disappeared at sea.

I started to think about how you just never know how the day will turn out. When your little boat leaves the harbour, what will happen next? Will it be a sunny day? Will you return with a large bounty of fish? Will you be hit by a storm that you didn't see coming? Will you navigate your way back safely? Or will your fate be sealed that day?

I have been caught in my fair share of storms. I have been blown about, and thrown off course. I have always been lucky to make it—sometimes feeling like I did so by the skin of my teeth. But I would stay at port for a while, wait for my energy and courage to return, and head back out. It is no life for me to stay at port. They say that a ship in harbour is safe, but that is not what ships are built for, and I hold to that belief.

I try to be wiser about when I head out, and about the reasons that motivate me. Sometimes I stay in when the conditions are looking too rough, or I choose another course. That's called discernment. Some days, I am a more skilful sailor than I used to be. Some days, I am not, still crashing into rocks.

But really, is it not a normal occurrence to encounter storms if you have the courage to take your boat out to sea? Instead of lamenting the encounter, how about being grateful that you made it through? Celebrate and take pride in the growing wisdom that you gain each time you do guide yourself through.

I use my self-talk to guide my ship out to sea, to give myself courage and comfort, and to go where my most inner voice guides me. That is how powerful self-talk can be.

My self-talk

- You can do it.

- Be courageous.

- Life is worth living fully.

- Everything is okay.

- I am here with you.

Wise words

"Above all, be the heroine of your life, not the victim." – Nora Ephron

The exploration: Stop telling yourself horror stories

When I lived alone, I decided that I would never watch horror films again. I thought that a woman living alone in a big city did not need any reminders of how scary the world could be. I wanted to feel comfortable and at peace in my home at night, which meant being mindful of what stories I allowed myself to hear.

It is the same with self-talk. If you want to keep yourself calm, retelling yourself the "horror" stories of your life and replaying the mini-dramas is not going to help you out. If anything, you will be stirring yourself up over and over again.

We can choose not to retell these stories, just like we can refuse to watch a movie. You simply must refuse to press the play button. When you catch yourself telling that story, stop it immediately. Press the stop button. There is nothing to gain by watching a movie that is scary or filled with conflict over and over again. To retell the story without any reason or objective is to hurt yourself.

If you are going to repetitively tell yourself a story, why not make it about the very best day of your life, or about a person that you find absolutely sparkling and lovely? Your whole system will love it.

In this exploration, I'd like you to see whether you have a horror story that you have told yourself over and over again.

What is the story? Does it serve you in any way to keep retelling it? Can you imagine putting that movie away and deciding to never let yourself watch it again?

If you do have a horror story, give it a title and write it down. Then boldly cross it out.

Now pick a joyful and delightful story that you can tell yourself instead. Write the title of this story.

From now on, each time you start telling yourself your horror story, press stop, and switch to your story of joy and delight.

A story that inspires me

Martine Rollin – "I said to myself: be brave. This was so important to me. It was like bright sunshine that called my name."

Martine Rollin is one courageous woman. Even when the world has seemed very scary, she has put on her big girl pants. After all kinds of major life challenges, she has gone onward and upward.

For many years, Martine kept an entire Harley Davidson wardrobe in her closet: boots, gloves, helmet, and leather jacket—even special sunglasses. They were the remnants of a long-gone relationship with a man who had a motorcycle. The two had taken long trips together, her riding behind him on the same motorcycle.

One day, she visited us from across the country, lugging all her gear as she was continuing on later to go on a bike trip with a friend. I was so surprised to see her collection. "I have always kept it," she said. "I love being on motorcycles so much. It makes me so happy. I hope the day comes that I meet someone with a motorcycle again."

"Why not get your own bike?" my husband piped up.

"Suddenly, it was like a light bulb went on in my head!" says Martine. "Why not, indeed!"

Still, there was a lot of fear to overcome. Fear of doing something new. Fear of the financial impact of owning a motorcycle. Fear of hitting the open road alone.

"I said to myself: be brave. This was so important to me. It was like bright sunshine that called my name," says Martine.

I am happy to report that if you see a beautiful, tiny, blonde woman riding an enormous Harley Davidson at full speed while smiling from ear to ear—you may be looking at Martine. Her next courageous challenge? She wants to fly Cessna planes.

My story: To stand courageously in my own power

Deep in the woods of Bowen Island is a 1,000 year old Douglas Fir tree they call Opa. Opa is huge, majestic, and strong, and a very rare tree. I had never seen anything quite like him. Standing in Opa's presence, I felt more calm. I felt more solid. His power inspired me. I wanted to be more like him: calm and powerful.

For me, personal power is about how I am with myself, how I stand in my truth, how I follow my own path with courage day by day. It is about my authenticity, my self-love, and my self-acceptance. And it is about how I keep all that safe.

Psychology Today has this to say about personal power:

"This type of power represents a movement toward self-realization and transcendent goals in life; its primary aim is mastery of self, not others. Personal power is more an attitude or state of mind than an attempt to manoeuvre or control others. It is based on competence, vision, positive personal qualities, and service."

One of my teachers told me recently that the loss of personal power is an inside job. When we start putting ourselves down, when we start to self-trash, our power seeps right out of us like a hole in a tire. It also happens when we let fear paralyze us. We just go flat.

I know what it is like to lose my power, to throw it away. This happens when I start telling myself, "You are not good enough."

Those words pull the plug right out from underneath me. They just drain me. I can feel my power and my energy leave in real time as I say those words to myself. Suddenly I am tired, worried, and anxious. My footing no longer feels secure. I get scared and I start to feel really small. These words do more to rob me of my personal power and energy than anything that happens to me from the outside. The loss of personal power really is an inside job.

When I feel the drain of energy and power, I stop and take stock. I notice what I have been saying to myself. Then I change the inner conversation. I choose words that make me feel courageous and powerful.

My self-talk

- I am powerful.

- I am good enough.

- I stand by me with my head held high.

- Be courageous.

- Be strong.

The exploration: Creating a new, courageous superhero voice

It is in your power to develop an inner voice that is filled with courage. This voice can grow in strength until it is very strong. It can help you feel courageous and stop fear from running your show.

That's what I did, and it works like a charm. I developed my own voice of courage, my own inner superhero, and her name is Mama Elizabeth. She is the voice I bring to the conversation when I am scared and need support.

My inner superhero Mama Elizabeth is creative in finding solutions, is resilient, and can handle most anything. She loves me unconditionally and is brave. I still invoke her every time the voice of fear starts taking over. I actively and consciously invite her to talk to me. She will say things to me like:

- It's okay. I can handle it.

- I don't know yet what solution I will find for this problem, but I can assure you that I will work it out.

- You just relax. I am on it.

- Everything will work out.

- This is no problem for me.

Now it's your turn to create a new inner superhero voice. You are going to invent this new voice, this strong, supportive, courageous and loving voice. At the beginning, you may need to call your inner superhero and have them talk to you deliberately. With time and practice, the inner superhero becomes part of your natural inner voices.

To start, let's imagine what she or he is like. You can imagine it, or base it on someone that you know, a person from popular culture, or a character from fiction who you admire (books, movies, history—it's all good.) Think of someone who inspires you.

Write down three qualities that this strong courageous person has.

Now give a name to your inner superhero.

What can your inner superhero say to give you courage and help you?

Wise words

"It takes courage to grow up and become who you really are." – *E.E. Cummings*

84

In closing: A last exploration

I invite you here to take some time to write, doodle, or draw images of your impressions of this chapter. What inspires? What triggers you? What do you embrace? What are your intentions for your self-talk? Can you imagine speaking to yourself with words of courage?

Choose your next chapter

In this chapter, you slowed down and said words of courage to yourself.

You can now choose to continue on the path that I've laid out and move to Chapter 7. In this next chapter, you will choose words of healing and well-being.

This is your journey. You can choose to move on to a different chapter and pause there for a while. Go where inspiration takes you. Trust your inner voice. Where does it want to go?

Chapter 7

Secure Your Own Oxygen Mask First

Or Choose Words of Healing

and Self-Care

Our intention with Chapter 7 is to choose words of healing and well-being.

You are one system. Your body and mind are connected. What you say to yourself influences your health, your well-being and your ability to heal. Everything that you say to yourself—whether positive or negative, life-affirming or life-denying—travels through your entire body and affects each one of your cells. Dr Candace Pert calls it the bodymind system.

Dr Pert discovered what are called neuropeptides, or messenger molecules. She found that your brain will transmit everything it hears and which creates emotion into a messenger molecule. Each messenger molecule carries a message of happiness or unhappiness in it.

For instance, if I tell myself that I am unlovable, that self-talk will create a molecule that carries a message of unhappiness in it, which then travels to every one of my cells. When my cells receive this message, they can actually shut down, affecting my entire immune system. The opposite is also true, though. When my cells receive a happy message, it tells them to be healthy and to perform their normal functions.

Be careful what you say to yourself because your whole body, your whole mind, your whole self, is listening.

My story: A pain in the neck

My neck had been jammed for several days. It hurt to move it and gave me a terrible headache. It was uncomfortable and I was in a big hurry to get rid of it. I visited the chiropractor and the massage therapist, stretched, applied heat, and popped Advil. I just wanted it gone.

This pain comes every few months when I am anxious or stressed, but this time when it came, I started asking myself why. What was the message that this jammed neck was telling me? What or who is giving me a pain in the neck? What is my body telling me?

Your body communicates with you. It is an awesome communicator. It may tense to tell you that something is wrong, or it may develop pain. It may show symptoms. It heeds to listen to them.

Dr Andrew Chin is my chiropractor. He has, many times, "unjammed" me, as I like to call it. Andrew is used to seeing patients who come to him in pain. Those who make an appointment when the pain is just starting are much easier to treat than those who have been ignoring the pain for many years. "Your body is telling you that something is wrong," says Andrew. "It is always a good idea to listen to it." I have started to wonder now if this neck pain could actually be a gift.

Quebec author and wellness expert Nicole Bordeleau calls such occurrences gifts that come in bad wrapping. They are sometimes the greatest gifts that we can receive, but we don't like the look of them. We don't like how they make us feel. We don't like the idea of what we need to do when they show up or how deep we need to go.

I used to call them dark gifts, but I am beginning to believe that they are all light gifts. How many times have I looked back on an experience that was painful and said to myself, "Thank goodness that happened?" I've thought this about a wide range of experiences, or gifts, from being dumped to getting sick.

They say that a messenger knocks softly on the door with a message. If you don't open the door, he knocks louder, and then louder, and then louder. The messenger won't go away until the message is delivered, and that may mean blowing open the door to force your attention. So all right, neck, what is your message for me? You won't have to blow the door off the hinges. I am ready to listen. I am ready to care for you.

My self-talk

- What is happening right now in my life that is giving me this pain?

- What do I need?

- What needs to be healed?

- What needs to be loved?

- What needs to be brought into my awareness?

The exploration: What is your body telling you?

Your body is wise and kind, and always wants to communicate with you.

Let's start with touching base with our bodies. Sit comfortably and plant both feet solidly on the ground. Take a deep slow breath. Let all the air out completely. Take another deep slow breath. Let all the air out completely. Bring your awareness inside your body. Keep taking deep slow breaths and letting all the air out completely. Stay in your body.

Is there any message that your body is bringing to your awareness? How long has your body been communicating this message to you? Your body's message is an invitation to give yourself more love and self-care. Would you like to accept it?

Wise words

"Meditation has been scientifically proven to activate the relaxation response, and as a result, almost every health condition improves." – Dr Lissa Rankin

A story that inspires me

Donna-Lynne Larson – *"The words I say to myself carry so much energy."*

Donna-Lynne Larson is the director, producer, and writer of a beautiful and insightful documentary called *Walk Talk Dance Sing: the movie about thyroid disease.* The basic message of her movie is that ignoring who you really are, not speaking your truth, and denying yourself the self-care that comes with living with joy can literally drain the life force right out of you. For Donna-Lynne, essential self-care includes walking, talking, dancing and singing—both literally and metaphorically.

The first part of the movie focuses on interviews with patients diagnosed with thyroid disease. We quickly realize just how debilitating this condition can be.

Walk Talk Dance Sing then takes a twist and ventures into the healing that comes with connecting with your deepest self. Donna-Lynne introduces a certain lightness by showing the magic that occurs when we give ourselves care by walking, talking, dancing, and singing. The movie celebrates what is possible when we honour who we really are and go with it. Says Donna-Lynne, "I focus on what is right for me. I am learning more and more about how to listen to my body. I trust that my body will tell me everything that I need to know. When I started listening to my own self, it felt very empowering. I could finally get my own answers. No one has this information for me but me."

The movie is also a testimonial to Donna-Lynne's own journey through thyroid disease to restored vitality and health. She says, "Before, I was looking on the outside for what can never come from the outside. Nothing was going to shift for me as long as I remained stuck in the victimizing pattern of external referencing. I changed the way I speak to myself. The words I say to myself carry so much energy. They are the precursors to my behaviours. Being mindful is everything."

My story: There is no better time than now for self-care

I heard a French song by Sandrine Kiberlain on the radio, in which she sang about caring for herself through running herself a bath, sending herself flowers, and keeping herself front and centre in her self-talk. Beautiful! I love how she gives herself permission to take the time she needs to focus on herself. She is creating a space where she can relax and be at the centre of her own story, where she can give herself the self-care she needs.

My friend David Holtzman told me that in the past, when he was really busy and stressed, he would tell himself to just get through this time so he could relax, care for himself, or enjoy his life later. Then he realized he was wishing his life away by always wanting to be in the future. Breaking the pattern, he began to give himself time to relax and enjoy his days no matter what was happening.

His words were a real eye opener for me, as I very often had said:

- Once this is finished, I will…

- Just get through this week and then…

- I don't have time now to rest, later when…

Most weeks were so super full. They went by quickly and I didn't give myself the care I needed.

The type and amount of care that I need really depends on where I am in my life. When there is drama, I am caring for others, or I am in pain, I need significantly more self-care. When life is going smoothly, I need a different kind of daily self-care, more like maintenance. On any given day, my self-care might include: drinking lots of water, playing, movement like dancing, walking, yoga, swimming, eating nutritious foods that taste good and give me energy, saying no, laughing, acupuncture, massage therapy, gratitude practices, spiritual practices, writing in my journal, or hot baths.

A form of self-care that I practice every day is to calm my nervous system. I meditate, do deep breathing, and take time alone to center myself when I start to feel anxious. It all helps my nervous system relax, and that, in turn, improves all parts of my life and my well-being.

Some even say that self-care is not an aspiration, but an ethical obligation.

I won't go into the details of all the times I harmed myself by not giving myself time and space for self-care, but suffice to say that no good ever came out of my neglecting it. Making space and time for fun, laughter, joy, well-being, and relaxation is part of self-care. Creating those elements in our daily life is self-care. David was the first one to show me how important that is. He found humour most everywhere.

It is a good thing that David didn't wait to live his life because it turned out to be short-lived. He died suddenly a few years ago. I still miss him.

My self-talk guides me, and reminds me that I am worth caring for—not only for me, but for those who love me and depend on my wellbeing. When I am well, living in the present, I have more energy and joy to share. With my self-talk, I give myself license to take good care of myself and my well-being.

My self-talk

- I love myself so I care for myself.

- I take the time to provide myself with a life that brings me well-being.

- I take good care of myself.

- My body heals itself naturally.

- I make choices that support my health.

The exploration: Self-talk and well-being

In this exploration, you will tell yourself words that celebrate your body's amazing ability to heal itself and the ways you care for your well-being.

This is a part of me that I am healing and caring for:

These are all the parts of myself that are healthy, vibrant, and strong:

These are some of the ways I take care of my health and well-being:

These are some of the ways I give myself joy:

This is how I care for myself when I feel anxious:

Wise words

"I have come to believe that caring for myself is not self-indulgent. Caring for myself is an act of survival." – Audre Lorde

In closing: A last exploration

I invite you here to take some time to write, doodle, or draw images of your impressions of this chapter. What inspires? What triggers you? What do you embrace?

What are your intentions for your self-talk? Can you imagine speaking to yourself with words of healing and well-being?

Choose your next chapter

In this chapter, we have explored words of healing, well-being, and self-care in our self-talk.

You can now choose to continue on the path that I've laid out and move to Chapter 8. This next chapter is about speaking to yourself in a way that guides you. You can become your own lighthouse with your self-talk.

This is your journey. You can choose to move on to a different stepping stone and pause there for a while. Go where inspiration takes you. Trust your inner voice. Where does it want to go?

Chapter 8

Be Your Own Lighthouse

Or Choose Words Of Guidance

Our intention with Chapter 8 is to slow down and choose words of guidance.

We often look to others for inspiration, for encouragement, or to show us what is possible and how to do it. I have been blessed with so many amazing teachers who have acted as guides for me when I have needed help or to be shown a way out of a difficult stretch. Some teachers I have studied with, while others have inspired me through their books and their talks.

We can also play that role for ourselves with our self-talk. We can be our own lighthouse pointing the way. You can direct yourself through challenging stretches. You can provide guidance to create the life that is right for you.

The intention in this stepping stone is to choose words that guide you, help you get where you want to go, and help you to become who you want to be.

My story: Being my own leader

When my daughter was a newborn, she woke up every few hours through the night. That is normal enough, but as time progressed, she started sleeping less and less. It became so extreme that she began waking up every hour. I was so sleep deprived that things were becoming dangerous. The final straw was when, in my tired haze, I didn't put the hand brake on properly, and my car rolled down the hill, crashing into our neighbour's brand new BMW. (Yikes! I have so much gratitude that only cars were hurt!)

I tried all kinds of books and techniques, and implemented advice from other moms to encourage my daughter to sleep. Nothing worked. One morning I just sat there completely discouraged, at a loss, my head hanging low, frazzled from yet another sleepless night. I wanted to give up.

Suddenly, I exclaimed, "What we need here is leadership! Leadership! Someone has to guide us out of here." I sat up taller. I became my own leader. I turned my gaze towards where I wanted to go, instead of where I didn't want to be. "I am going to take care of this. Don't worry. I will figure it out. There is a solution out there. We just need to find it. This will pass and soon everyone will be sleeping."

I gave myself a briefing as to where we were headed, and what our plan was. "We all need to sleep way more. We will find a solution that works for our family. We are going to find that solution and it is going to work!" Then I let it go, trusting that I would indeed find a solution.

That was the boost I needed that morning. Re-energized, I found another book that provided just the advice we needed, and consulted with a child therapist. Before long, we were sleeping again.

My self-talk

- You can do this.

- I am taking charge here. I will take care of it.

- You have solved much bigger problems in your life. You can handle this too.

- Get as much rest as you can for now. Simplify your life until things are more normal.

- I know we will find a solution.

The exploration: The briefing

When I had my PR agency, my clients expected me to come up with solutions to problems, big and small, every day. I also had to conjure up creative ideas for media campaigns. Many times, I initially didn't know what to do. What I would do is "brief" myself like a good leader would, and then trust that my unconscious mind would find a solution or idea for me.

This is how I did it:

I told myself all the details of a client or campaign in the same way that I would explain it to someone else. Then I literally told myself that I was looking for a solution or idea. After that, I let it go and went to do something else. Suddenly, in the shower, during a walk, or during a swim, boom! It would come to me. Then I would scramble to write it down because the same idea may not come twice.

Letting go is key to this process because the part of the brain that wants to find a creative solution for you needs time to consider things. It works on its own timeline, and it has trouble doing so if you are trying to force an answer out of it.

Want to give it a go?

Start by briefing yourself. Tell yourself all the details of a situation—don't skip anything, and don't assume that you "already know." Keep all the information positive and as objective as you can. Brief yourself on the 5Ws of the situation: the who, what, where, when, and why.

Next, clearly ask yourself to find a solution or come up with an idea. Assign it to yourself. I am looking for a solution to: _____.

Now—importantly—let it go. Go on and do something else. Trust that your best person is on the job. Let it take its course.

Wise words

"Accept your light and let it shine to create your own lighthouse on a stormy night." – Pauline Duncan-Thrasher

A story that inspires me

Marie-Josephine Pon-An – "When days were difficult, I told myself that they would just pass. I was not going to let negative self-talk stop me."

Marie-Josephine Pon-An had every reason not to go back to school and start a new career. Her financial resources were limited. Her family had recently immigrated from the Philippines and needed a lot of her time to settle in. She was well into middle age and wondered if it was not too late.

Any one of these challenges would be enough to discourage many individuals from starting a new career, but Marie had a dream. Ever since she was a little girl, all she had wanted to do was to become a chef. She decided to go for it, even though the odds were against her.

Says Marie, "I really wanted to do it for self-fulfillment. I wanted to show my children an example of how you can strive in life. I said to myself that I can change my life. I can do it."

Making up her mind was the first step of a difficult journey to complete her studies to become a chef. The going got tough. The hours were long at school, and she had to work in the evenings to make a living. It was difficult, physically, to stand for hours on end in the kitchen. She was often exhausted and sleep-deprived in caring for her family, going to school, and working. There were times when she wondered why she was putting herself through it.

But every time she wavered, she told herself that she could do it. That she could continue through obstacles. That life would get easier. She also stopped herself from talking to herself negatively. "When days were difficult, I told myself that they would just pass. I was not going to let negative self-talk stop me," she adds.

She also used a visualization technique. She saw herself climbing a mountain. She took it one step at a time on the mountain, telling herself she was climbing and would get to the top. She kept her eyes on the summit. She talked herself through the journey. She told herself over and over again that she could do it, to keep climbing day by day.

And you know what? She did make it to the top. Marie now works cooking delicious pot pies in a production kitchen, and she loves it. "I am happy and so proud of myself," she says.

To be your own greatest supporter is a gift that you give yourself on the journey to the top of your own mountain. I draw inspiration from those like Marie, who work hard on the climb, and who show courage and vision when the going gets tough. They encourage me to keep going on my own journey. The climb to become the genuine and authentic you is not always an easy one. Self-talk and visualization can be powerful tools in helping you grow into the real you.

My story: A season for everything

When I left Japan after five years, I was sad to say sayonara to the cherry blossoms. I had fallen in love with them at first sight, and my enthusiasm had only grown over the years. I really loved the tradition of sitting under the trees, enjoying the petals, and spending time with friends and colleagues.

More than just an annual party, the cherry blossoms are also a symbol of what the Japanese call "mono no aware"—or the transience of things. It speaks of the impermanence of everything, that there is a time for everything, that everything comes and goes and passes.

When I left Japan, I thought that was it for cherry blossoms. As spring approached, I lamented the fact that I wouldn't be seeing any that year. Little did I know that I was living on a cherry blossom-lined street, in a new city filled with them. I didn't know because for most of the year, the cherry blossoms look like every other tree out there. And then for 14 days or less, they explode in delicate, beautiful petals, growing from thin and tentative to a full, extraordinary explosion of pink. For such a short time, they have all eyes on them, emanating and eliciting joy to all who notice them. The rest of the time, they rest, blend in, lose their leaves, and stand bare.

Aren't we a little like that? The cherry blossoms remind me that there is a season for everything. Sometimes it is your moment to shine to the world, other times your moment to rest, heal, recharge, and reconnect with yourself. You can't just bloom all the time. You can't be go, go, go, always on show, always building, always trying to get somewhere or get something done. There are times to let go of old ideas, ways of being, or habits that no longer serve us. There are times for healing. There are times for rest. There are times to go into the darkness where roots grow, and find meaning there.

You can guide yourself with your self-talk. You can help yourself understand where you are and what is needed in this time in your life. That is being your own lighthouse. Instead of fighting like crazy with what life is asking of you—especially when it goes against your plans for the day or for your life—what if you go with the current and the seasons of your life? What if you trust the naturalness of your own life?

My self-talk

- What is there for me to notice right now, at this moment in my life?

- What good can I see in this situation right now?

- What needs to be done now?

- What needs to be let go of now?

- How can I guide myself?

Your turn to explore: The power of intention

Everything that we create in life starts with an intention.

Intentions are a very powerful way through which we communicate with ourselves. They let our entire being know in which direction we are headed. We are our own leaders when we set the tone for our journey with an intention.

If you are inspired, I invite you to spend a few moments thinking about what are your most precious intentions towards creating your right life, towards being at ease with who you are. You can focus on any aspect of your life. What calls you right now? Do you want to create? Do you want to change in some way?

This is what I create in my life:

This is who I want to be:

This is how I want to feel:

This is what no longer serves me and I release:

Feel free to write additional intentions that call you right now.

Wise words

"Following our inner guidance may feel risky and frightening at first, because we are no longer playing it safe, doing what we 'should' do, pleasing others, following rules, or deferring to outside authority." – Shakti Gawain

In closing: A last exploration

I invite you here to take some time to write, doodle, or draw images of your impressions of this chapter. What inspires? What triggers you? What do you embrace? What are your intentions for your self-talk? Can you imagine becoming your own lighthouse and using your inner speech to guide yourself?

Choose your next chapter

How excellent that you are speaking to yourself with words of guidance. Your self-talk can show you the way.

You can now choose to continue on the path that I've laid out and move to Chapter 9. This next chapter is about choosing self-talk that protects you—even from your own negative and cruel voices.

This is your journey. You can choose to move on to a different stepping stone and pause there for a while. Go where inspiration takes you. Trust your inner voice. Where does it want to go?

Chapter 9

Keep Yourself Safe Even From Your Own Self

Or Choose Words Of Protection

Our intention with Chapter 9 is to slow down and choose words of protection.

What does it mean to grow up, and to become a real adult? It is about having the maturity to become the one where the buck stops. Synonyms of maturity include thrive, flourish, develop, grow, and bloom.

As the grown up, you also become the protector of those you love and all that you honour. It means protection from others or situations that are harmful, but also protection from your own inner voices that may be cruel or excessively critical. By choosing words of protection in your self-talk, you begin to feel safe inside your own self.

My story: Protection from the inner bully

I once had a conversation with a woman, whom I had known at university, on a day when I was sad and vulnerable. I had recently suffered a miscarriage, and I was in a bad way. I told her of my troubles when she called. She made light of my feelings, and then proceeded to remind me of all the mistakes I had made and all the relationships I had failed. She kept it jokey in her usual irreverent style, but I knew she meant it. If I had thought I was down before our talk, I reached a new low after our conversation. It was like she had given me a push closer to the precipice into which I was already staring.

Worse than her words was the fact that I didn't defend myself, and even worse, had started to agree with her on the inside. My inner bully was triggered by what she said. Just as I didn't protect myself from her, I let the inner bully go for the jugular. I started to say terrible things to myself. "She is right. I have made so many mistakes in my life. It's my own fault. That's why this is happening to me. I don't deserve to be happy. I don't deserve to be a mom. There is something wrong with me and I can't have what so many others have."

In a time when I was so in need of compassion and kindness, I was cruel and merciless to myself. I let the inner bully have a field day with me. I did not courageously come to my own defence.

Now that I know how speaking to myself cruelly affects me, when I catch the bully speaking to me that way, I stop her in her tracks. I stop listening to her. I stand up and protect myself. I choose words that put protection and love in.

My self-talk

- What you say is not true, and I don't believe you.

- Enough now with this talk.

- I know I am a good person.

- Enough. You are lying.

- I will not listen to you anymore.

The exploration: The Circle of Protection

I invite you now to protect yourself from the words of your inner bully by creating a Circle of Protection around your heart.

Draw a heart. Now draw a Circle of Protection around this heart. Imagine that it only lets in love, and that all words that are cruel, fear-based, and negative bounce right off the Circle of Protection. They cannot come into your heart.

Outside the Circle of Protection, in very small letters, write a message that your bully tells you. Then cross it out.

Inside the Circle of Protection, write a message of love and protection to counterbalance what the bully says.

Wise words

"I know that each of us must care enough for ourselves that we can be ready and able to come to our own defence when and wherever needed." – Maya Angelou

A story that inspires me

Leslie Matheson – "With this self-talk, I was able to comfort myself."

This is how it used to go down for Leslie Matheson when her inner critic reared its negative head.

One night, Leslie found herself alone in a hotel room in a strange city. The next day she was to start a new career in the wine industry. Instead of feeling excited and happy that her dream of many years was coming true, she was anxious. As she lay in bed, she listened to the voice of her inner bully go on and on about all that could go wrong. It belittled her, telling her she was not capable of succeeding. "You don't belong in this industry. You don't know what you are doing. You are not good enough. This is too risky. You will lose your home. You'll end up living on the streets. You won't make it." By the time her inner bully had finished with her, she had worked herself up so much that her back began to spasm from stress.

This is how she describes the situation:

"It opened my eyes to the horrors of negative self-talk and how my body reacts to my negativity by seizing up. From then on, my self-talk was much more positive and reassuring: support, kindness, love and affection. My back does not seize when those are my pillars."

Now, when the inner bully decides to pay a visit and tries to sabotage her, Leslie challenges it. "The other day the bully said something to me that was so cruel and so degrading that it shocked me. Instead of listening as I used to, I told her to stop it immediately. That it wasn't true, that I was a good person. With this self-talk, I was able to comfort myself."

Wise words

"Caring for your inner child has a powerful and surprisingly quick result: Do it and the child heals." – Martha Beck

My story: Taking care of my inner child

When I was nine years old, a neighbour of my grandmother tried to sexually assault me. I was in a friend's barn feeding chickens when he came at me with his pants down. I was able to hit him with the feed bucket and run away. I ran like crazy until I reached my grandmother's house up the country road. When I got there, my family and relatives were at the table eating lunch. I didn't tell anyone what happened. I was too ashamed. I didn't trust anyone enough to reach out for help. I just sat at the table, and cried.

I was very lucky to have escaped. Years later, this man was arrested and jailed for sexually assaulting many other children. I know that I was lucky and that it could have been much worse. Yet, it still altered my life. I know that inside me, that nine-year-old still lives, and that she is scared and hurt. I tried to bury her deep within me, but she is there under all the layers—like she is caught in a time capsule.

There are messages that she told herself that day that I can still hear inside—sometimes only whispers, other times much louder, if she is triggered. She says to herself that the world is scary. She thinks that she can only depend on herself. She says that she is unsafe.

When I get anxious or freaked out, it is a sign that my inner child is distressed, scared, and freaking out inside.

I thought that growing up meant growing out of the inner child. As it turns out, it doesn't. Being an adult means you start caring for the inner child, and protecting her with strength and kindness. Now that I understand that she is there, I can give her what she needed that day: protection and love. She now has me, a grown, powerful woman who is her protector, her ally, and her parent.

I cannot erase what happened to her, but I can hold that little girl's hand, hug her, and talk to her inside myself. I comfort her and calm her down when she needs it. She feels so much calmer when I do.

Self-talk for my little girl:

- You are safe.

- I love you.

- You belong here.

- I will always love you and I will always be here with you.

- I am here to protect you. My job is to protect you, and I am really good at it. You can relax. Everything is okay.

Exploration: Protecting the inner child

We all have a little child inside us who only wants love and protection. Now this child has a powerful new ally: you. You are now grown. You are powerful. You know how to love. You are now in a position to give this child everything that she/he needed back then.

Let's go back in time to hold our inner child and tell her/him what she/he most wants to hear. Write down what you, as the loving protector, want her/him to know.

In closing: A last exploration

I invite you here to take some time to write, doodle, or draw images of your impressions of this chapter. What inspires? What triggers you? What do you embrace? What are your intentions for your self-talk? Can you imagine speaking to yourself with words of protection?

Choose your next chapter

In our self-talk, we can choose words that put protection in. We can choose to speak to ourselves in a way that makes it clear that we cherish and protect ourselves. That's what we just explored in Chapter 9.

You can now choose to continue on the path that I've laid out and move to Stepping Stone 10. This next chapter is about choosing words that help you calm down, that help you relax.

This is your journey. You can choose to move on to a different chapter and pause there for a while. Go where inspiration takes you. Trust your inner voice. Where does it want to go?

Chapter 10

When In Doubt, Take A Nap

Or Choose Words Of Calm And Relaxation

Our intention with Chapter 10 is to slow down and choose words that calm and relax our systems.

Life is meant to flow through you. You want to be like a cat in the sun, not like a cat hanging from the drapes. Do everything you can to relax, to feel a sensation of ease in your body, mind, and spirit. When you are relaxed, and your nervous system is calm, it's like the world opens up and you see more goodness and solutions. When you feel tranquil, you can hear your own voice more clearly guiding you. The only way to relax is to pause.

In the pause, we can hear our own voices. In the pause, we can figure out what our life means to us, or where we want to go next. In the pause, we can figure out meaning. In the pause, we can plan for how we want to live next, for who we want to become. In the pause, we can put love in.

The words I say to myself help soothe my wary nervous system. They tranquilize me. My self-talk helps me relax so I can be myself, hear myself, and lead my right life.

My story: A day I got frazzled and it only got worse

After a long day at a workshop, I decided to treat myself to a night in a bed and breakfast, to save myself the commute and to get a good night's sleep. I was feeling spent after the long day working intensely with a group. As a highly sensitive person, I can feel frazzled and drained after being with a group, even when it is a great experience.

I was looking forward to a quiet, solitary dinner at a little English pub, and then a stroll in the woods to further relax. The B&B owner had different plans for me, and she graciously insisted that I join their dinner party that evening. My entire being wanted me to say no, but it was such a heartfelt invitation that I accepted. Plus, the food looked really good.

Much later, I headed out for a walk in the neighbourhood. I called home to say good night to my daughter and caught her in the middle of a tantrum. After I calmed her down, I thought, "Okay, now it's my turn to relax." I walked down a little path, turned a corner, and came face to face with a big black bear. I ran all the way back.

I was now completely revved up. It takes about 20 minutes for an over-aroused nervous system to calm down. I didn't give myself that time. When I get off my axis, I start to crave all kinds of things that ultimately don't make me feel any better. This is a common reaction. After the long day, the dinner party, the tantrum, and the bear, I ended up watching trashy TV for hours and eating the chocolates in my room. I didn't follow any of my regular practices to relax my system. I was too thrown off to want to get back to centre.

When I finally went to bed, I tossed and turned all night, and woke up exhausted.

It could have played differently. It is never too late to guide myself back towards the centre of myself, where I feel peaceful. With my self-talk, I can say no to activities that make me feel even more stressed, and go towards practices that relax me, like a hot bath, a peaceful walk, yoga, stretching, soft music, meditation, or deep breathing. I can give myself that time and space that I need to calm down.

I can also talk myself into going to spend time with people with whom I feel relaxed. That's the case when I visit my meditation group. Being around people who are meditating calms me right down—even if my own mind is racing. That's because there is a process called "entrainment," where your body synchs up with the rhythms and beats of other people. Being around calm people is calming.

Being around people who are anxious and are doing nothing about it has the opposite effect. Their anxiety is contagious to me.

Looking back, I wish I had given myself permission to say no to the dinner party, and had provided my nervous system what I knew it needed: time alone to wind down. A beautiful thing about life is there is always a next time to get it right.

My self-talk
- I am going to help you calm down.
- I give you permission to stay home quietly, even if the invitation sounds fun. I need rest.
- I am saying no because I love you.
- Tell me about today. Let's sit here together quietly. I will listen to you.

- What do you need right now? What will make you feel calmer?

Wise words

"The time to relax is when you don't have time for it." – Sydney J Harris

The exploration: Mantra breathing to calm the system

Believe it or not, when you breathe, you are communicating with yourself. When you take a deep breath, you are telling your brain that you are okay. When your breathing is shallow, you are telling yourself that you are in trouble. Just taking a few deep breaths tells your nervous system that everything is all right and that it can calm down. When you need to relax your system, it can be even more powerful to attach a mantra to your breathing.

Dr Shimi Kang recommends being realistic with yourself, but also positive. For instance, your self-talk can go along these lines if you are frightened:

"I know you are scared. It will be over soon."

As you breathe in, you are realistic. ("I know you are scared.") As you breathe out, you encourage yourself. ("It will be over soon.")

It's your turn to create your own breathing mantra.

Is there anything you are presently experiencing around which you could use a little relaxation?

Write a message for your in breath (the realistic one).

Write a message for your out breath (the encouraging one).

Now, practice saying your messages as you breathe in and breathe out slowly. Practice it again and again until you feel your system relax.

A story that inspires me

Camilla Ravindran – "Gratitude helps me be at my highest. It makes me feel at peace."

Camilla Ravindran is a mother, a wife, and a coach who guides women all over the world to be empowered by their feminine energy and their inner goddess. One of the most powerful rituals in her life is her gratitude practice. She practices it herself, and also encourages her clients to do so. "Gratitude helps me be at my highest. It makes me feel at peace. Gratitude from the heart is not just a practice, it's a state of being. When we are in that state, magic happens naturally," says Camilla.

The first thing that Camilla does every morning, upon waking, is count her blessings. She tells herself about three things she is grateful for. "It is such a powerful way to start the day. The challenge is to not let it be an automatic thing, but to be present and let the gratitude rise from within."

At the beginning, she found it challenging to find three things. "With time, it became easier and easier, being able to be grateful for the smallest things, like the smell of flowers during a walk." After several years of a daily practice, Camilla began sharing it with the world via Facebook. "I thought that it could inspire others to think of the blessings in their own lives." And it certainly has. Countless individuals have been lifted by her attitude of gratitude and have started a practice of their own.

Here are some of her recent gratitude musings:

- "I am thankful for my breath and the ability of my body to move and its health. I am blessed and thankful."

- "I am thankful for yoga and silence, for the healing. I am blessed."

- "I am thankful for morning smiles and games, cuddles, pancake breakfast, rain."

- "I am thankful for the trip to the farm, the beautiful animals, the laughter, and kids playing."

And it is not just the so-called "good things" that Camilla counts in her blessings. She believes all that comes into our lives is for beneficial reasons. "Everything is part of gratitude—even what we perceive as the 'dark' gifts because there are none. It all comes to us from love," she adds.

Wise words

"When all else fails, take a nap." – Unknown

My story: Oh, what a beautiful morning! Start the day with gratitude and positive self-talk

It is 5:30 a.m., and the alarm rings. I throw on the clothes I put next to the bed, pull on my raincoat, slip on boots, and head out into the cold, rainy morning. It is so dark that it could be the middle of the night. Morning after morning, I faithfully drag myself out of bed to do this—no small feat for me. For one whole hour, I walk around the deserted streets and beaches. I am so determined, even on the worst stormy mornings. I am starting my day with gratitude and positive self-talk.

When I started this practice, my stress levels were shooting through the roof at work and in my personal life. My first thoughts upon waking were generally about how tired I was and how I hadn't slept enough. I immediately moved on to think about work and what I had to do that day. I was starting my days focusing on scarcity, stress and negativity.

It dawned on me that rushing out the door and grabbing breakfast on the go probably wasn't helping how I felt. I came to believe that I needed a morning ritual that set the tone for a more peaceful, joyous day. There is something very sacred and powerful about how you start your day. You are setting the tone for the entire day.

127

What you say to yourself has a big impact. It starts a momentum that just keeps going. Every morning is like a reset button. During my walk, I told myself all the things and the people I was grateful for. Some days I woke up feeling crappy, and it was a stretch for me to think of anything I was grateful for, so I went for the small things: thankfulness for rubber boots in the rain, for having a warm bed, for my apartment near the ocean.

As I continued doing my ritual morning after morning, I became much more relaxed. Telling myself what I was thankful for made me feel like I had abundance in my life. All was going to be okay. I felt stronger, more calm, more solid.

I don't run out the door anymore, but I still have a morning ritual to start my day positively, with gratitude. As I wake up, I tell myself about the happiest things I can, people or events that have a very high joy factor for me. I tell myself about the love that I have in my life. I think of how great my dog Egli was, the funny things my daughter says, my grandmother hugging me when I was under quarantine for a communicable disease, snorkelling in Hawaii, the text from my friend, my husband holding my hand. I am as specific as I can be. I revel in the details of this loving self-talk. I start a momentum in myself of positive self-talk, of gratitude, and of calm. I can feel the abundance in my life. My system is relaxed and I am ready to start another new day. Who knows what joy it will bring?

My self-talk

- Thank you for living in a beautiful city.

- Thank you for the good night's sleep.

- Thank you for all the people that I love and who love me.

- Thank you for my mom's cooking.

- Thank you for having a home where I can be safe and rest.

The exploration: The gratitude list

Research has shown that keeping a gratitude journal increases your happiness by ten percent—that is the same percentage as if your income was doubled. Tell yourself what you have to be grateful for. It can be little things, like "I have a warm sweater on," or "I ate a good breakfast." Let your self-talk be about what you want to offer thanks for. A simple list of three to five items will do—or lots more, if you are inspired. Let yourself feel it. Tell yourself about it. Feel it as deeply as you can. Celebrate the blessings in your life.

Here are some ideas for a gratitude list:

- The people I love

- My most cherished blessings

- The places where I feel happy

- The abundance in my life

- The foods I enjoy

- The times I laugh

- All the parts of my body that are healthy and strong

- What I love in my home

- The visionaries, leaders, and kind people I am grateful to be sharing the planet with (even if I don't know them personally)

Go ahead, and explore many others if you would like.

In closing: A last exploration

I invite you here to take some time to write, doodle, or draw images of your impressions of this chapter. What inspires? What triggers you? What do you embrace? What are your intentions for your self-talk? Can you imagine choosing words that help you relax?

Choose your next chapter

In Chapter 10, you slowed down and chose words that help your nervous system calm down and relax.

You can now choose to continue on the path that I've laid out and move to Chapter 11. This next chapter is about speaking to yourself in a lighter way, in a more humorous way. You can choose self-talk that will elevate you.

This is your journey. You can choose to move on to a different stepping stone and pause there for a while. Go where inspiration takes you. Trust your inner voice. Where does it want to go?

Chapter 11

Lighten Up, Baby

Or Choose Words Of Levity And Humour

Our intention with Chapter 11 is to slow down, and choose words of levity and humour.

What we say to ourselves is either life-affirming—brings you more of the good stuff, like love, calm, compassion—or it is life-denying—taking you further away from the good stuff. Humour and levity help you choose self-talk that is life affirming. They elevate us, help us rise. They help us turn towards the light just like plants do on the window sill. As soon as you choose humour in your self-talk, a joyous part of you shows up for this better time. What relief!

Make up the most funny and light story that you can about whatever you face in your life. Make yourself into a comic character instead of a dramatic one. Write about it. Talk about it. Draw it. Chant it. Sing it. Turn yourself towards the light.

My story: Laugh it right out of me

I was on a train, years ago, feeling very sorry for myself, and crying over the problems that had befallen me. The friend I was travelling with turned the situation on its head. He said something so surprising and funny that I burst out laughing. Although my problems were not solved, I felt better, lighter, less like a tragic heroine. He gave me such a gift that day when he made me laugh. He helped me elevate.

Using levity and humour is a powerful way to use your self-talk to feel more at ease in the world. It doesn't mean that you are not respecting or honouring situations, it means that you can also see and feel light when there would only be darkness.

Humour and love are there in the painful, dark circumstances. I was very close to my grandfather and was very sad when he died. I never would have guessed that I would find his funeral so funny. We were sitting in the pews of the chapel, crying, when an ancient priest began to deliver a eulogy so insane that it shocked us right out of it. We all stared back in disbelief. At the reception, we laughed so hard recounting the absurdity and I suddenly felt all the love I had for my grandfather. Oscar was a very humorous man—always making jokes, seeing the funny everywhere, and giving people amusing nicknames. He would have loved the crazy speech. I wouldn't put it past him to have sent the priest to remind us to lighten up.

Laughter has such a way of elevating us. Finding levity in a situation, if not outright humour, is the gateway towards joy. Imagine a line. Negativity is below the line, and positivity is above the line. Levity and humour are ground zero. Levity and humour are what permit us to lift ourselves above the line. Thinking lighter—even slightly comical—thoughts permits us to rise. It can get a new momentum going. Think lightness. Think of a hummingbird: light, free, comical, joyous.

Laughter is an opening into love. As Leonard Cohen wrote: "There is a crack in everything. That's how the light shines in."

The crack for me is humour.

My self-talk

- Be lighter.

- What can be funny about this?

- It is okay for you to be light and silly and to find humour everywhere you can.

- Life is such a gift, and life wants us to enjoy that gift to the max. Laugh, my love, laugh.

- You are my funny girl. I love you even when you are in a tizzy.

Your turn to explore: Top 5 funny moments

Top 5 lists are a great way to talk to yourself about a topic. Top 5 lists can cheer you up, remind you of what is important, and help you see the lighter side of life. Pick topics that are fun to explore and will elevate you: the top 5 funny people you know, the top 5 good times in your life, your top 5 favourite places. Here is my Top 5 list of big-belly amazing laughs:

- In 10th grade math class with Charlie—sorry Mr Salome!

- In church right before a recital of the Messiah

- On the phone with my husband

- With my dad, watching Jane Campion's movie "Sweetie"

- With my friend Helene after her daughter's baptism

Now it's your turn.

A story that inspires me

Trilby Jeeves – "I try to remind myself to see the funny side of things. It is really useful for everyday life."

Trilby Jeeves teaches buffoonery workshops. The buffoon is a little like the court jester, laughing at life with all its absurdities. In these delightful workshops, you get to bring out your inner fool, the irreverent, hilarious, funny, and ironic you. Trilby calls her workshops "the cure for serious." She is an ace at leaving no stone unturned until you find the freedom to be wacky. She is an inspiration to many of us who take things way too seriously.

Humour has helped Trilby get through many hard days. She recounts a time when her mother was in the hospital and her father in a wheelchair because of his advanced multiple sclerosis. She had to pack up their apartment and move them both into a care home. The task was enormous and she felt discouraged under the heaviness of it all. Suddenly, she found a moment to lighten up. She spontaneously launched into a funny buffoon like character with a New York accent who talked about the trials of packing and moving. Both she and her father cracked up. "Laughter can get us through a lot," she says. "Levity permits us to see a lighter side and maybe find solutions. That helped dad and me. It helped us through some tough emotions."

Adds Trilby, "I try to remind myself to see the funny side of things. It can be really useful in everyday life, like when I am driving and have a mini road rage moment. I catch it. I imitate myself getting all worked up, and tell myself, 'Oh, there you go, being so serious and angry at the other driver.' Then I have a chuckle and away goes my stress." She admits that it's an ongoing practice, and she loves it when a friend or colleague taps into the buffoon way and makes her laugh.

My story: Letting go of what no longer serves me

I once spent the whole night climbing Mount Fuji, in Japan. The goal was to get to the top by sunrise. I was a totally inexperienced mountain climber, a city girl who frankly didn't know what I was getting myself into. I was miserable, and close to tears most of the night. My friend and I had gone on the very last weekend before the mountain was closed for the season. There was a freezing wind blowing from what I imagined could only be Siberia. The climbing was steep and hard.

I had on a heavy backpack that only got in my way. I don't remember what was in it, but it didn't contain anything that could be useful for my journey, like yummy snacks to comfort, goggles to protect my eyes from the blasting wind, hot tea, or warmer clothes. I would have been better off just abandoning the backpack.

I sometimes feel like I am carrying a backpack filled with rocks of all sizes, representing all the pain that I have felt and am hanging on to. Some are old stories that I still tell myself. Some are old beliefs that I no longer need. Some are my reluctance to forgive and move on. Some are little pebbles, and others are big boulders. The backpack weighs a ton and I don't want to carry it around with me anymore. It digs into my shoulders, hurts my back, and robs me of energy that I could use in many other wonderful ways. It hampers my ability to take life lightly, to find the funny in life.

I am ready to take some of the stones out, take a look at them, learn what they are there to teach me, heal what calls to be healed, thank them for their service, and let them go. Bye, heavy load. Hello, footloose freedom! What if it is true that everything that happens in life happens for me, and not to me?

I am freeing myself so I can have more joy, more laughter, more lightness, more space in my heart for love, and more energy to create my right life.

My self-talk

- What no longer serves me?

- What can I release?

- It's okay to let go.

- You are even safer without this heavy load.

- I trust you.

Your turn to explore: Find the funny

One day, my friend had a headache and went into a supermarket to buy water with which to take aspirin. She slipped on the wet floor and fell, smashing her head badly enough that they had to call an ambulance. Nothing funny there, you think? Well, when she told me the story, we both burst out laughing when we realized that if she had a headache going into the store, it was nothing compared to the headache she had going out. We saw a very funny twist in it.

Is there a story you are telling yourself about something in your life that could use a little lightening up? Let's see if you can bring levity to it with your self-talk.

Pick a situation you are dealing with in your life that you don't find especially funny.

Write it down.

Now see how you can lighten it up.

Is there anything about it that can be comical? Amusing? Ironic? Even strange? What can you say that will bring a little levity to the way you talk to yourself about it? Maybe there is something funny about the way you handled it, or the drama you are bringing to the situation, or how worked up you are about it.

Rewrite your story with its new comical twist.

In closing: A last exploration

I invite you here to take some time to write, doodle, or draw images of your impressions of this chapter. What inspires? What triggers you? What do you embrace? What are your intentions for your self-talk? Can you imagine choosing words of humour?

Choose your next chapter

In Chapter 11, we explored what it would look like to choose self-talk that elevates you with levity and humour.

You can now choose to continue on the path that I've laid out and move to Chapter 12. This next chapter is about slowing down and listening to yourself. The most important part of any communication is in the listening.

This is your journey. You can choose to move on to a different chapter and pause there for a while. Go where inspiration takes you. Trust your inner voice. Where does it want to go?

Chapter 12

I Can Hear You

Or Choose Words That Show You Are Listening

Our intention with Chapter 12 is to slow down, and choose words of listening.

I spent years of my life making sure that I didn't listen to myself. I only paid attention to myself or listened when the message got too loud to ignore. I stopped working only if I got sick. I broke off relationships when they became unbearable. I wasn't paying attention to my body, my mind, or my spirit.

I was a stranger to myself. It was exhausting and very stressful to be on the run from my own self. How could I know what my truth really was, or who I was, if I didn't listen? I have no idea what goes on with the people I love unless I listen to them. To know where my loved ones are at, I must pay attention and listen carefully. Same goes with me. When I listen to myself, I feel connected. When I don't take the time, I am alone.

Life can be hard at times, but going through it alone is harder. Being disconnected from myself, and ignoring myself, means I am essentially alone.

My story: Listening to the ways I communicate with myself

When I worked at someone else's PR agency, the owners hired a consultant to train us to be more efficient. The consultant advised us to stand when someone entered our office. By standing, you send the message that you are busy and don't have much time, or any time, to give your visitor. We were pushed to work more, and produce more, at the expense of listening to each other, and of our relationships.

With my self-talk, I don't want to communicate with myself like I was trained to speak to my colleagues: on the fly, and on the surface. When I stop all my multitasking, my activities, my work, and my care of others, and sit with myself for even just a few minutes to touch base, it tells me that I care for myself, that I love myself.

When I listen to myself, I tell myself that I am important. I am worth spending the time with. I feel heard, acknowledged, accepted, and loved. Plus, I get to receive very important information that helps me navigate my life and know what to do.

It's amazing how many ways we communicate with ourselves: our feelings, our sensations, our bodies, our gut feelings and intuition, our sensitivity, our breathing, our inner speech. We are like a multi-media communication campaign, sending self-messages in all kinds of ways. The information I receive through these channels is so valuable. What I hear is my truth. It doesn't mean that I always like what I hear. It can be highly inconvenient, or even devastating to what I have already created. It doesn't even mean that I know what to do about the information I get. It is, however, my truth, and I am always served by honouring it. In the same way that I honour what my loved ones tell me, just listening is powerful in itself. I feel calmer, purely by being heard.

When I listen to myself, I hear all kinds of amazing wisdom, from what I really want, to what my body needs to be healthy and filled with vitality.

My self-talk

- What I have to say to myself is valuable and meaningful.

- I take the time to listen to myself.

- I trust my own voice.

- I trust the truths that I communicate with myself.

- I am listening.

The exploration: Intuitive writing

Intuitive writing is a good way to listen to a part of yourself that you don't hear from very often. When you write with your non-dominant hand (for example, your left hand, if you are right handed), it taps into a different part of your brain. You access your creative, intuitive mind. The answers generated are different than when you write with your dominant hand, where you are in touch with the logical and rational part of your mind.

When I explore intuitive writing, the handwriting is all over the place and it is slow going, but I am amazed at the answers that come from inside me. Often, I didn't see them coming.

Want to give it a try? Answer these questions using your non-dominant hand. Be open to what wants to be heard.

- How am I?

- What do I need in my life right now?

- What do I most need to know?

- What do I love?

- What am I curious about right now?

- What needs to be changed?

- What brings me joy?

- Who brings me joy?

Explore some of your own questions.

Wise words

"Listen to your own voice, your own soul, too many people listen to the noise of the world, instead of yourselves." – Leon Brown

A story that inspires me

Lori-Ann Speed – "My intuitive voice is an infinite source of wonder and amazement, guidance and wisdom for me."

Lori-Ann Speed is a classical pianist and composer. She also has an amazing ability to hear her own intuitive voice, and she uses it to help her clients in one-on-one reading sessions. She has developed this skill over many years of listening to herself. She shares the wisdom of her intuition in both her music and in her sessions. Both are designed to awaken, heal, and transform. Her piano compositions, such as "A Sacred Beauty" and "Nature Speaks," incorporate spoken ancient wisdom and rich piano compositions.

Lori-Ann says that her intuitive voice is one of her greatest joys. "My intuitive voice is an infinite source of wonder and amazement, guidance and wisdom for me. It is beyond my mind. It is wisdom that comes to me from my highest self." She adds, "It guides and informs me all the time. I am constantly connected to my 'still, small voice.' Whether I choose to listen to it all the time is another story. But it is always there, always available. No special time or place needed. It is a constant companion. My intuitive voice can tell me anything I ask it. It can answer any question posed to it."

She seeks the counsel of her intuition for matters big and small in her life, whether it is what road to take, or what to do. "But also, my intuitive voice is just always transmitting, even without a direct question. It is a constant source of guidance, from where to find things that are lost, to generating choices that create synchronistic events and outcomes. I chose to contact a person I had not spoken to for three years because my intuitive voice guided me to call. He came up in my awareness for several days, and I knew it was a call to contact him. I did and we met. He was in need of support and healing in his life. It was an important meeting and my intuitive voice guided me to it."

Lori-Ann says that we all can develop our intuitive voice. "It just takes a capacity for deep listening. It takes practice to hear it and to trust it, to have confidence in it. My intuition continues to grow and expand. I have a deeper and deeper connection with it and I feel confident about it now in a way I didn't when I first began. It is something that I will probably continue to learn about for the rest of my life. If I can do that, so can you."

Wise words

"The more you listen to yourself, the more you will hear. Your awareness will grow. It is like a bird watcher. You see birds everywhere once you start paying attention." – Ran Fuchs

My story: The voices on the bus

On a walk one day, I met a woman with a big sweet dog named Charlie. As Charlie came to say hello, the owner explained that the dog was part Labrador, and part Beagle.

"Beagle?" I asked, thinking the big dog looked nothing like one.

Beagles are famous for making a howling sound. Apparently, Charlie shocked herself the first time she howled. She jumped around to see what had made that noise. She hadn't known she had the Beagle voice inside her.

It's a little like that for us. There are voices inside that we have yet to discover. We may have never heard them. They may be little whispers that are easily ignored. We may have decided long ago to bury them deep, out of shame, and never use them. But they are there waiting for us to listen to them.

Now imagine that all these voices are riding a bus together, and that you are the bus driver, the one in charge of the whole operation. A few of these voices sit in the best seats up front. They talk to the bus driver

149

continuously. They tell the driver what to do and where to go, and evaluate the driver's performance. They are your dominant voices. The voices in the front seat can be positive, or they can be negative. They can be loving and kind, or critical and nit picky. They can help you make your dreams come true, or sabotage them.

The helpful, friendly, and kind voices will praise and love the bus driver. They will give her compassion even when she takes a detour. They are friendly, helpful, and generous, and they give the driver the encouragement she needs on difficult journeys. They say messages like this:

- You are doing a good job.

- I trust you.

- Everything is ok. Just keep going.

- I will help you reach the destination.

- I love you just the way you are.

- You are getting better.

- Good job! That was a tricky situation you just navigated.

Now imagine if the front of the bus is filled with negative voices. These bullies give terrible advice and put down the driver constantly. They drown out the kinder voices coming from further back. They say messages like this:

- You are not good enough.

- You don't know what you are doing.

- You can't do anything right.

- There is something wrong with you.

- You will never make it.

- Everybody else drives better than you.

How can the driver focus on the road and reach the destination—much less feel good about herself—under such circumstances? In some cases, the critical voices grab the steering wheel and drive the bus, while the driver sits silently in the back, having lost all power.

As the bus driver, you want to always stay in charge of your bus. You are the driver, you are not one of the passenger voices. You get to decide which voice you want to listen to, and whose counsel you will follow. Never forget that you are the consciousness who listens and who decides where the bus will go.

It is even in your power to promote one of the voices from the back of the bus and give it a prize seat up front. As the Tibetan spiritual teacher Chögyam Trungpa wrote: "You hold the wheel of command."

I have given a prime upfront seat to my voice of kindness and self-compassion. She once sat in the last row, and now she sits right behind me, supporting me. For now, the critic still sits in the seat next to her, but her voice is not as loud. My kind voice has brought a new balance to my life. I am much calmer, thanks to her.

My self-talk

- I am none of these voices. I am the one who listens to them.

- I get to decide which voice I want to listen to and whose advice I want to follow.

- I have the choice to empower a new voice and promote it to the front of my bus.

- Which voices do I want to listen to more?

- What do I most need in my life? How can I give it to myself?

The exploration: Voices on the bus

Would you like to explore some of the dominant voices that sit in your bus?

Start by writing your name in the top centre of a piece of paper. You are the bus driver—firmly in power and in control of your own bus.

Beneath your name, write the names of one or two voices who occupy the front seats. Go ahead and invent a name for them.

Do any of the voices sitting up front give you unconditional love? Friendship? Compassion? Kindness? Encouragement?

If yes, hooray!

If not, let's promote one from the back of the bus. We all have voices of love, friendship, compassion, kindness, and encouragement sitting somewhere on our bus. You can promote one from the back to the front.

Now grab a new piece of paper. In this new bus, again put yourself in charge as the bus driver by writing your name in the top centre of the page.

Now promote a voice to the front of your bus.

Write its name in the space right behind you. It is there to support you.

Now I invite you to write a message you would like to hear from this voice.

In closing: A last exploration

I invite you here to take some time to write, doodle, or draw images of your impressions of this chapter. What inspires? What triggers you? What do you embrace? What are your intentions for your self-talk? Can you imagine taking time to listen to yourself?

The end of this journey

In Chapter 12, we slowed down to listen to our own selves—to show ourselves that we are worth listening to.

If you have followed this book chapter-by-chapter as I've laid it out, then you have come to the end of the journey. I hope some of these stories and explorations are like little seeds that you can tuck away in your heart, and that can take root.

Thank you for taking this time with me and for reading my stories. If you liked the experience, come find me online as I continue my own exploration of what it means to speak to myself with more love.

We may also meet in person one day at one of my workshops.

With gratitude and much love,

Maryse

www.selftalklove.com

Facebook: selftalklove.com

Little Extras: If You Want To Know More

Women featured in "A story that inspires me"

Trilby Jeeves
www.trilbyjeeves.com

Donna-Lynn Larsen

www.studiowild.ca

Camilla Ravindran

Facebook: Camilla.Ravindran

Lori-Ann Speed
www.lori-annspeed.com

Maggie Howell
www.natalhypnotherapy.co.uk

Jacky Yenga
www.jackyyenga.com

Cecile Gambin
www.cecilegambin.com

Leslie Matheson
Facebook: Thewinewhisperer

Self-talk and the brain

If you think that it doesn't matter how you talk to yourself, think again. This is an exciting time for self-talk because research and science are able to prove the theories that have been circulating for decades. We are now able to neuro-image self-talk. It turns out that one part of your brain—part of you—listens and responds to everything the other part says. It is truly like an inner conversation. Your brain reacts to what it hears. Your brain responds the same way to negative self-talk as it does when someone else is criticizing you. This means that if you are belittling yourself or emotionally abusing yourself, then you are causing as much damage as if someone else were doing it to you. Even if you don't realize what you are saying to yourself, part of you is hearing it all and is affected by it.

Where some of the inner voices come from

According to the work and theories of psychologist Lev Vygotsky, some of our inner voices were created by what we heard as children. The way your parents and caregivers spoke to you became ingrained inside you. These voices were internalized before your fifth birthday. They are not really your true inner voice. When you speak to yourself cruelly, when you criticize yourself, or when you withhold love in your self-talk, that is not the way you were built to be. Our birthright is to have inner love and self-talk that is kind and loving. Your parents and caretakers did the very best they could at the time with what they knew and who they were. Now it is up to you to transform your self-talk into that which will support and love you.

More on why it is good to calm your mind

A very powerful form of self-talk is what you say to yourself unintentionally all day long. It is the non-stop chatter that can go on and on in your head, with you often not even aware of it consciously. My friend calls it the head DJ, as it is like a radio playing in the background. Most of the time you don't realize what is being played, and then every once in a while you notice the song that is on, and you think, "Man, I love that song," or, "That song sucks." Imagine the toll that such interminable self-talk has on you, especially if your inner speech tends to be negative, critical or cruel.

Buddhists call this the monkey mind, as it jumps crazily from one thought to another. This is what your mind does. This is its job. Sometimes these waves can take on an incredible momentum and may seem unstoppable.

With our self-talk to help us relax, we can give ourselves a chance to calm the mind.

Relax by going into your body and out of your mind

Eckhart Tolle suggests that the best way to get out of your busy mind is to get into your body. He suggests focusing on your hands, and feeling the energy in them. With your conscious mind, go into your hands. It is the most immediate way to get out of your head and to slow the waves down. This is one way to practice what is called mindfulness, which means to be aware of what is going on in the present moment.

More on gratitude and its benefits

Robert Emmons is a gratitude researcher, and the author of several books on the subject, including *Gratitude Works!: A 21-Day Program for Creating Emotional Prosperity*, and *Thanks! How the New Science of Gratitude Can Make You Happier.* He says the benefits of a gratitude practice are wide-ranging, and include a stronger immune system and better sleep.

More on the benefits of levity and humour

Taking yourself less seriously and laughing more may help protect you against a heart attack. Michael Miller, M.D., of the University of Maryland Medical Center, says laughing every day is good for our hearts. "We don't know yet why laughing protects the heart, but we know that mental stress is associated with impairment of the endothelium, the protective barrier lining our blood vessels. This can cause a series of inflammatory reactions that lead to fat and cholesterol build-up in the coronary arteries and ultimately to a heart attack," he says.

What you tell yourself with your feelings

In her book *The Art of Empathy: A Complete Guide to Life's Most Essential Skill*, Karla McLaren writes about how all our feelings have messages they are communicating to us. She says that you want to develop a deep empathetic relationship with your own feelings. For instance, when you feel angry, you are telling yourself that one of your boundaries has been crossed. When you feel sad, there is something not working that needs letting go.

Making the ultimate commitment to yourself

In her TedX talk called "The Person You Really Need To Marry," writer Tracy McMillan discusses the importance of accepting yourself and loving yourself as you really are. Self-love is not about saying to yourself, "Oh, if only you hadn't done that, I could love you. If only you had not made that mistake, I could love you." Self-love is for better or worse, and accepting the full package of yourself. Love is accepting all of you, your whole self, as you are, as you show up, at all moments.

Highly sensitive people and self-talk

Highly sensitive people (HSP) are able to hear very subtle messages. My sensitivity is always communicating with me. I get information about the people, places, and experiences I come into contact with. It can get pretty intense in a room full of anxious, angry, or fearful people. Conversely, it can be an absolute joy to be in the presence of someone who is relaxed and happy.

Dr Elaine Aron has written many insightful books about highly sensitive people. They are a treasure of scientific information on the trait, as well as tips on how to cope with all the information your brain processes as an HSP.

Self-talk and creativity

Researchers have found a strong link between creativity and self-talk. Namely, when your self-talk is negative or dysfunctional, it gets in the way of your being able to think creatively. When you are busy putting yourself down and doubting yourself, your mind has less time and energy to search for creative solutions to the challenges you face. Those who employ constructive self-talk that puts them in a positive light are more able to inspire themselves—and others. Eric Maisel is a psychologist and creativity coach. He writes, in his book *Coaching the Artist Within*, that negative self-talk can block your creativity. He suggests replacing negative inner speech, such as "I can't do it" and "It feels too difficult," with affirmations, such as "I am ready" and "I am capable and courageous."

Self-talk and happiness

In her book The Happiness Track, Emma Seppälä, of Stanford University, writes that changing your self-talk from one of criticism to self-kindness can transform your life. "Research shows that self-criticism is basically self-sabotage, whereas self-compassion—treating yourself with the understanding, mindfulness, and kindness with which you would treat a friend—leads to far greater resilience, productivity, and well-being."

More on developing a new inner voice

Creating an inner superhero, to get through hard times or enable you to face what scares you, is a practice held by many. When Jane McGonigal was injured and had a serious concussion, she created an inner superhero to help her heal and deal with the emotional repercussions of being immobile in a dark room. Her book is called *Superbetter: A revolutionary approach to getter stronger, happier, braver, and more resilient.*

Positive self-talk and your health

Negative self-talk can really take a toll on you, your well-being, and your health, while positive self-talk can support you in being healthy, peaceful, and at ease in your life. The Mayo Clinic states that positive self-talk can provide a host of health benefits, including a longer life (that may be the ultimate benefit!), less stress, and feeling better physically and emotionally.

About The Author

Maryse Cardin is an author, workshop leader, university instructor, communications practitioner, and coach. She is dedicated to speaking to herself with love, compassion, and kindness, and to helping others learn to do the same. Her passion for teaching positive and loving self-talk is driven by her desire for everyone to have lives filled with love, health, calm, joy, and fulfilment. For many, self-talk is the key to healing and personal transformation. Meet Maryse at www.selftalklove.com and facebook: selftalklove

In Gratitude

There are many generous and kind souls who helped me get this book out into the world.

To start at the beginning, a loving thank you Maman and Papa for getting me started on this adventure that is my life.

To all my students, workshop participants and readers – I am thankful for your trust.

I am grateful also to all the women featured in this book who shared their stories with me. You inspire me to keep blooming.

My husband Robert lovingly supports me in all my projects. For that and many other reasons, I am grateful to share my life with you.

My daughter Eloise enthusiastically cheers me on and gives me inspiration. Having her opens me to love everyday. Thanks Eloise!

Avital – you are a talented designer and I am lucky that you created such a beautiful book cover for me. Thank you!

Thank you, thank you, thank you Lucy for bringing talent, humour, and your editing skills to the table. I could not have written this book without you.

Laurie and Ran, thank you for reading my manuscript and giving me loads of worthy advice.

My proof-reader Sara really was born with a red pen in her hand. Thank you!

29467904R00096